In our unsettled and polarized [...] by the solutions offered by th[...] our heads in the sand. Bird and Wright remind [...] Jesus truly is king and the hope of the world, and they encourage us toward steady faithfulness when it is easy to be swept away by the shifting winds of historical and political circumstance. Read this book, remember 'the old story,' and pursue public faithfulness while resting in truth.

VINCENT BACOTE, professor of theology, director of the Center for Applied Christian Ethics, Wheaton College

In *Jesus and the Powers*, N. T. Wright and Michael F. Bird draw on a wide array of historical, biblical, and theological resources to offer a much-needed contribution to discussions regarding Christian faith and politics. They present a broad theopolitical vision of how the church should relate to empire that will exhort, challenge, correct— and at times likely provoke—their readers. Their arguments reach an international audience and transcend the particularities of contemporary politics to point readers back to the heart of Christian life and witness: serving Jesus our king and advancing the kingdom of God.

AMY E. BLACK, professor of political science, Wheaton College

At a time when discussions about Christian nationalism and debates over religion and politics too often involve more heat than light, *Jesus and the Powers* offers something different. Drawing on their expertise in biblical theology and on two millennia of global Christian history, Tom Wright and Mike Bird present a defense of liberal democracy that pushes back against the extremes of the Left and the Right. There are no easy answers here, but readers across religious and political spectrums will find much to grapple with in this sharply written text, and perhaps also a framework for the pursuit of mutual human flourishing in a polarized age.

KRISTIN KOBES DU MEZ, professor of history, Calvin University, author of *Jesus and John Wayne: How White Evangelicals Corrupted a Faith and Fractured a Nation*

Tom Wright and Michael Bird's individual contributions to New Testament scholarship, church life, and practical Christian living are immeasurable. This dynamic duo teams up again to draw attention to the relevance of Jesus and the Bible for our divided and fracturing world. Unthinkable only a decade ago, the very fabric of democracy is under threat. What was once stable and reliable is now in danger of collapse. Although this may be new to us today, it is not new to God's people. In some ways, topics and emphases in Scripture that were important for the earliest church are now relevant again. Wright and Bird help us reorient ourselves to implications of the gospel message for today's climate. Topics discussed include the kingdom of God, power, and the relationship between the church and secular authority. Wright and Bird's purpose is neither to promote some political agenda nor inform Christians how to vote. Circumstances and the Bible demand a more nuanced approach. Rather, they wish to help us understand the implications of the gospel for our daily interaction with the world and to act accordingly. In the end, this is a call for Christian action and a source of hope for the church today.

JOSEPH D. FANTIN, professor of New Testament,
Dallas Theological Seminary

The rise of Christian nationalism in the United States, the rise of Buddhist nationalism and the coup in Myanmar, Russia's invasion of Ukraine, and the Israel-Palestine conflict all pose moral challenges in how Christians should faithfully witness to Jesus as the global lord of freedom. N. T. Wright and Michael Bird, whose lives have both been shaped by world empires in some way, have written a timely book on Jesus and the powers. Using the Bible as source and the kingdom of God as a theological foundation, they innovatively demonstrate how Jesus and his disciples' political witness against powers in the first century should be used as a contextual guide for the contemporary church's public witness against political powers of the regimes for the common good in the twenty-first century. This brilliant book is a fresh contribution to New Testament political theology today. It offers readers a nuanced understanding of the relationship between Christ, the kingdom, the church, and politics. This book is academic yet accessible, political yet pastoral. I highly recommend it to anyone working in the global academy, grassroots church, and public society.

DAVID THANG MOE, Rice postdoctoral associate and lecturer in Southeast Asian Studies, Yale University, review editor, *International Journal of Public Theology*

In a time when Christians face pressure to either remain silent about God's kingdom or conquer their opponents in its name, Wright and Bird call the church to choose neither. Christians have a vital role to play in politics at all levels of government. Yet as Wright and Bird explain, those who bear the name 'Christian' represent Jesus in their service and sacrifice, boldly speaking truth to power when necessary, neither in dominating their neighbors nor capitulating to evil. Can Christians defend pluralism and liberal democracy and remain faithful to King Jesus? Not only is it possible, Wright and Bird explain why they must.

SAMUEL L. PERRY, professor of sociology, University of Oklahoma, coauthor of *The Flag and the Cross: Christian Nationalism and the Threat to American Democracy*

Wright and Bird help us situate where the church sits between presidents and principalities. Keeping politics out of Christianity is impossible, for Christianity is inherently political. Too many books on politics shortchange the biblical text. This book brings you back to the first century and then back again to the twenty-first century with tools pertaining to our public witness.

PATRICK SCHREINER, associate professor of New Testament and biblical theology, Midwestern Baptist Theological Seminary, author of *Political Gospel: Public Witness in a Politically Crazy World*

An excellent, short pilgrimage in biblical political theology! With divisions and animosities running high within and among nations and with autocrats increasingly in charge, we need this book acutely.

MIROSLAV VOLF, professor of theology, Yale University Divinity School, founding director, Yale Center for Faith and Culture

Almost every Christian today struggles at some level to understand the political implications of the gospel: What have kingdom concerns to do with cultural crises, or the good news with the daily news? Under what circumstances is civil disobedience warranted? Can a Christian wholeheartedly support any political system? In *Jesus and the Powers*, you will find Mike Bird and Tom Wright neither fence-sitting nor drumbeating, but guiding Christians thoughtfully, practically, and jovially through a minefield of contemporary political and social questions with a careful commitment that draws deeply on the wisdom of the Bible.

CHRISTOPHER WATKIN, associate professor of French studies, Monash University, author of *Biblical Critical Theory: How the Bible's Unfolding Story Makes Sense of Modern Life and Culture*

Jesus and the Powers helps us think clearly and deeply about what Christians are called to be and do in our present day. It casts a vision that takes seriously God's call to engage in the work of service, sacrifice, and reconciliation to the benefit of everyone around us—in Wright and Bird's words, to 'build for the kingdom.' Any fellow Christians wrestling with the question, 'Where do we go from here?' would do well to receive what is shared within these pages.

ANDREW L. WHITEHEAD, associate professor of sociology, Center for the Study of Religion and American Culture, Indiana University-Purdue University Indianapolis, author of *American Idolatry: How Christian Nationalism Betrays the Gospel and Threatens the Church*

This is an ambitious book of the sort that only two seasoned theologians and (equally important) true lovers of Jesus could conceive of and write. And it is a book Christians need in this time of war, political turmoil, and threats to human flourishing around the world—many of these, the fruit of arrogant earthly empires. What should the church's response be to such profound brokenness? And what should the response of individual Christians be? The book's arguments marry political theology with sound history, both ancient and modern, all to show that 'the kingdom of God is not from this world, but it is emphatically for this world.' History shows that other lords and kings will rise and fall, trampling others underfoot in the process, but there will always, only be one lord and king. And that is a call to action for us all.

NADYA WILLIAMS, author of *Cultural Christians in the Early Church: A Historical and Practical Introduction to Christians in the Greco-Roman World*

Jesus inaugurated his ministry by proclaiming the coming of the kingdom of God. What does that long-ago event have to do with us today? Everything, say the authors of *Jesus and the Powers*. The fundamental character of authentic Christian political activity, they argue, is 'building for the kingdom.' Using their skills as esteemed New Testament scholars, the authors first illuminate what Jesus would have meant by 'the kingdom of God' and then explore how present-day Christians can build for the kingdom. I know of no other book that comes even close to locating, so insightfully and in such rich detail, Christian political activity within the context of the coming of the kingdom. Given what is happening in politics today, their call for Christians to engage as workers for the kingdom could not be timelier.

NICHOLAS WOLTERSTORFF, Noah Porter Professor Emeritus of Philosophical Theology, Yale University

Many Christians are asking afresh whether the Bible can be helpful for us in the 2020s to be fully committed followers of Jesus, on the one hand, and yet also be engaged in the political realm, on the other hand. The authors of this book have spent much of their lives attempting to understand the New Testament and here bring their decades of academic expertise, accumulated wisdom, and Christian convictions to bear on some of the most difficult but relevant questions at this nexus today, in particular how the church should retain its witness to the gospel while interfacing with the state and its various kinds of governments. Their invitation to explore what faithfulness means between Christian separatism and Christian nationalism is a gift especially to believers that hold Scripture to be normative for Christian faith and practice in a pluralistic world.

AMOS YONG, professor of theology and mission, Fuller Seminary

JESUS AND THE POWERS

Christian Political Witness in an Age of
Totalitarian Terror and Dysfunctional
Democracies

N. T. Wright and Michael F. Bird

ZONDERVAN
REFLECTIVE

ZONDERVAN REFLECTIVE

Jesus and the Powers
Copyright © 2024 by The Society for Promoting Christian Knowledge. Text by Tom Wright and Michael F. Bird.

Original edition published in English under the title *Jesus and the Powers: Christian Political Witness in an Age of Totalitarian Terror and Dysfunctional Democracies* by:

SPCK
Publishing part of SPCK Group
London, England, UK
www.spck.org.uk

Published in Grand Rapids, Michigan, by Zondervan. Zondervan is a registered trademark of The Zondervan Corporation, L.L.C., a wholly owned subsidiary of HarperCollins Christian Publishing, Inc.

Requests for information should be addressed to customercare@harpercollins.com.

Zondervan titles may be purchased in bulk for educational, business, fundraising, or sales promotional use. For information, please email SpecialMarkets@Zondervan.com.

ISBN 978-0-310-16226-1 (audio)

Library of Congress Cataloging-in-Publication Data

Names: Wright, N. T. (Nicholas Thomas), author. | Bird, Michael F., author.
Title: Jesus and the powers : Christian political witness in an age of totalitarian terror and dysfunctional democracies / Tom Wright and Michael F. Bird.
Description: Grand Rapids, Michigan : Zondervan Reflective, 2024. | Includes bibliographical references and index.
Identifiers: LCCN 2023046432 (print) | LCCN 2023046433 (ebook) | ISBN 9780310162247 (paperback) | ISBN 9780310162254 (ebook)
Subjects: LCSH: Christianity and politics. | Power (Christian theology) | BISAC: RELIGION / Christianity / General | RELIGION / Christian Living / Social Issues
Classification: LCC BR115.P7 W75 2024 (print) | LCC BR115.P7 (ebook) | DDC 261.7—dc23/eng /20240126
LC record available at https://lccn.loc.gov/2023046432 LC ebook record available at https://lccn.loc.gov /2023046433

Cover design: Darren Welch
Cover photos: © rasslava / Getty Images

Printed in the United States of America
24 25 26 27 28 LBC 6 5 4 3 2

Contents

Preface   xiii

Abbreviations   xviii

1 The Kingdom of Jesus in the Shadow of Empire   1

2 The Church between Jesus and Caesar   25

3 Power and the 'Powers' in Early Christianity: John,
   Paul and the Paradox of Biblical Politics   40

4 The Kingdom of God as Vision and Vocation   74

5 The Church between Submission and Subversion   103

6 The Church Resisting the Powers of Today   122

7 Liberalism and Love in a Time of Fear and Fragmentation   150

8 Conclusion   174

Index of Biblical References and Ancient Texts   179

Index of Names   183

N. T. Wright is research professor emeritus of New Testament and early Christianity at the University of St Andrews and senior research fellow at Wycliffe Hall, Oxford. He is the author of more than eighty influential books, including *The New Testament for Everyone*, *Simply Christian*, *Surprised by Hope*, *The Day the Revolution Began*, *Paul: A Biography*, *The New Testament in Its World* (with Michael F. Bird) and *Into the Heart of Romans*.

Michael F. Bird is deputy principal and lecturer in New Testament at Ridley College, Australia. He is the author of numerous scholarly and popular books on the New Testament and theology, including *A Bird's-Eye View of Luke and Acts*, *Evangelical Theology*, *Jesus among the Gods* and, with N. T. Wright, *The New Testament in Its World*.

Preface

We, Tom and Mike, enjoyed our collaboration with SPCK and Zondervan in writing *The New Testament in Its World: An introduction to the history, literature, and theology of the first Christians* (2019), as well as the spin-off video series *The New Testament You Never Knew* and the masterclass lectures put out by Zondervan. We find again a common interest in our concern for how to 'build for the kingdom' in an age of – as the front cover says – totalitarian terror and dysfunctional democracies. We have both dipped our toes into this area before, Tom with his book *God in Public: How the Bible speaks truth to power today* (2016) and Mike in his *Religious Freedom in a Secular Age: A Christian case for liberty, equality, and secular government* (2022). We are not trying to be political theorists or social activists, but we are concerned with the political and social implications of the gospel. The globe is awash with terror, tyranny and trauma, divisions and despair, not just in the West, but also in Asia, Africa and the Americas. Our world seems dangerously combustible, due to financial crises, pandemics, increasing injustices and inequalities, democratic chaos, geopolitical upheaval, wars and rumours of more wars to come.

The aim of this book is not to be like most publications on Christianity and politics. We are not going to tell Christians what they should think about abortion, gun control, Brexit, Trump, climate change, racial justice and other hot-button issues. But neither are we offering an abstract theory of statecraft and faith-craft that never quite comes in to land in real life.

Jesus and the Powers has one objective: to say that, in an age of ascending autocracies, in a time of fear and fragmentation, amid carnage and crises, Jesus is King, and Jesus' kingdom remains the object of the Church's witness and work. That is true today, tomorrow, the next day, until death and despots are no more, until such a time when 'he has put all his enemies under his feet' (1 Corinthians 15:25). Such a conviction means that the Church needs to understand how it relates to empires biblical and burgeoning, how to build for the kingdom in our cities and suburbs; to understand the time for obedience to the State and the time for disobedience to the State. We need to grasp where the Church sits between presidents and principalities. We must think deeply as disciples, without partisan prejudice, unbeguiled by the deceptions of demagogues, in order to attain 'every good thing that is at work in us to lead us into the Messiah' (Philemon 6). We want people to consider how we can pursue human flourishing, how we might work towards a common good, and how we can pursue the things that make for peace in a time of political turmoil such as has not been seen since the 1930s.

We hope that such a book will help Christians begin to discern how to respond with wisdom to the situations in places such as Ukraine, Nigeria, Gaza, Myanmar and Taiwan. Help them to discern how to think about constitutional monarchy and democratic republics. Teach them to fear the seduction of political power. Call them to seek to build something that carries over into the new creation, as well as to rest in the goodness and faithfulness of the one who is King of kings and Lord of lords.

To such ends, our book begins by noting the political upheaval and emerging empires of our own day. It then describes how Jesus and his followers came on to the scene at the height of the Roman Empire and had to negotiate their own way around various imperial horrors (chapter 1). Thereafter, we point out that the Church had to pivot from being under the threat of the empire to enjoying its many benefactions. The Church's relationship with emperors, and then with kings and princes in the Middle Ages, fashioned a host of complications about Church and State relations with which we are still living today. Christianity brought about a revolution in European civilisations and is now part of the political and moral DNA of the West. But the Church was also party to unholy alliances with Western rulers, not least in its complicity with European empires that wrought colonial violence all over the world. Yet whatever the good, bad and ugly of history, the Church cannot retreat from politics. If we are to speak truth to power and stand up to the powers, then we must do kingdom-business with the business of political power (chapter 2).

On the topic of the 'powers', these loom large in the scriptural narrative, with spiritual and political forces intersecting across the tapestry of history. Looking at Paul's letter to the Colossians and especially at John's Gospel, we see that the powers of this age will be pacified by Jesus and then reconciled through him. The back story here is that God had always intended humans to be partners in his dominion. Yet the powers of the age fomented rebellion and wreaked havoc so that creation itself now groans for deliverance. God's solution is to telescope authority into one human being, one child of Abraham, one Israelite, one son of David – the Messiah. His death makes atonement for sins and brings a victory that results in the ruler of the world being cast out and the powers of darkness being disarmed. In the here and now, governments might have power; but they are merely granted power, and they will be held to account for how that power is exercised.

The Christian vocation is neither pious longing for heaven nor scheming to make Jesus king by exerting force over unwilling subjects. Instead, Christians should be ready to speak truth to power, being concerned with the righteous exercise of government, seeing it bent towards the arc of justice and fulfilling the service that God expects of governing authorities (chapter 3).

Following naturally on from that point, we must address more concretely the topic of how to build for the kingdom in what is becoming a frightening and fraught world. The kingdom might not be *from* this world, but it is most certainly *for* this world, so we cannot retreat from the world with our kingdom-mission. So, we proffer some suggestions as to what building for the kingdom looks like in actual practice (chapter 4, which reworks several of Tom's lectures, articles and resources from his books *God in Public* and *How God Became King: Getting to the heart of the Gospels*).

We next discuss the topic of submission to governing authorities (chapter 5) and when Christian witness requires us actively to disobey them (chapter 6). These are difficult and complicated subjects, and we are concerned to affirm the goodness of government as much as to explain what we might do if governments revert from public service to predatory tyranny. Finally, we set forth the case for a liberal democracy. It is the 'liberal' in 'liberal democracy' that enables us to live with political and cultural differences, not despite being a Christian but precisely as a Christian. Nothing is straightforward, diversity breeds conflict, but we are called to love our left-wing and right-wing neighbours, and to build a better world for people of all faiths and none (chapter 7).

That is the journey that lies ahead of readers. It is something of a short pilgrimage in political theology, undertaking a mixture of biblical overview, zooming in on church history highlights, centring on Jesus among the powers, offering reflections on Church–State relations, and wrestling with knotty topics such as 'secularism' and 'civil disobedience'. The task is about trying to think and pray through the missional vocation and kingdom witness of the Church in our contested political theatres. The Church carries a gospel which is not reducible to this-worldly political activism, nor so heavenly minded as to live aloof from the trials and terrors of our times. If the gospel announces that 'Jesus is King', then we must wrestle with what Jesus' kingship means in Tiananmen Square, on the floor of the US Congress, in the lunchroom of Tesco or Walmart, or in choices we make at the ballot box. There will be a day when politics is no more, when all things are subject to 'the kingdom of our God and the authority of his Messiah' (Revelation 12:10). Before then, we need wisdom, for the Church has much work to do to prepare for such a day.

Finally, we remain grateful once again to Philip Law of SPCK for guiding this book through to completion and for his advice and feedback along the way. The Zondervan team led by Katya Covrett was also a wonderful part of the cast of characters who helped in the publication of this volume. Brian Walsh was kind enough to offer feedback on parts of the manuscript. Unless otherwise specified, all New Testament translations are from Tom's *The New Testament for Everyone*, 3rd edition (London: SPCK; Grand Rapids: Zondervan,

2023), while the Old Testament translations are taken from the New Revised Standard Version Updated Edition.

Tom Wright and Michael F. Bird

Postscript

This volume was in its final stages of pre-production just as the Israel–Gaza war began in October 2023. We lament the loss of innocent life and the carnage and cruelty that has taken place. The present conflict has deep and murky roots, resulting in a politically and morally complex situation which intersects with colonialism, empire, land, religion, violence, human rights and wider geopolitical factors. It is almost impossible to say anything about this subject without inflaming someone somewhere. The brutality of the Hamas attacks on Israeli citizens reminds us of Isaiah's denunciation of those who 'rush to shed innocent blood' (Isaiah 59:7); yet we concede that Israel's treatment of the Palestinians over two generations also reminds us of King Ahab's violent seizure of Naboth's vineyard (1 Kings 21). Alas, the powers are again doing their worst, bringing horror and bloodshed to Israelis and Palestinians alike.

With Israeli hostages still being held in Gaza, and Palestinian children dying in the streets, there is no time to waste on partisan antics or grandiose statements for tribal consumption. We urge all readers to challenge dangerous rhetoric, whether it concerns driving Jews out of the land 'from the river to the sea' or, conversely, treating the Palestinians in Gaza as the 'Amalekites' who should have been wiped out long ago – in both cases appearing to invoke biblical precedent or even warrant for the ongoing cycle of violence and wickedness.

Abbreviations

Calvin, *Institutes*	Calvin, *Institutes of the Christian Religion*
Gregory of Nyssa, *Hom. Eccl.*	Gregory of Nyssa, *Homilies on Ecclesiastes*
Josephus, *Ant.*	Josephus, *Jewish Antiquities*
Josephus, *War*	Josephus, *Jewish War*
LXX	The Septuagint, a Greek translation of the Hebrew Bible
NT	New Testament

1

The Kingdom of Jesus in the Shadow of Empire

History strikes back

'I was born in a country that no longer exists.' When I (Mike Bird) tell people that, they give me odd looks, as if I was maybe born in Atlantis or Narnia. But I assure them that my place of birth is not the stuff of myth or fantasy. After letting them make a few poor guesses I soon put their confusion to rest by clarifying, 'I was born in the Federal Republic of Germany or West Germany for short.' The Federal Republic of Germany (FRG) came into existence because of a string of empires that rose and fell before it: the Kingdom of Prussia (1701–1871), then the German Empire (1871–1917), then the Weimar Republic (1918–33), then the German Reich (1933–45). After the Second World War, the country was partitioned into West and East Germany (1945–90), and then, after the Berlin Wall came down, the country was again unified as a new entity (1990).

I (Mike) was born in Germany because my father was serving in the British Army as an armoured cavalry soldier as part of the British occupation of post-war Germany. Then, when I was 4, my parents divorced, and my mother and I moved to Australia, a former British colony, a direct legacy of the once-great British Empire. She married my stepfather, who was the son of Serbian immigrants who came to Australia after the Second World War because of the ethnic violence that plagued the Balkans. Note too that Australia had been a part of the British Empire since the time of colonisation (1788) and federation (1901). However, since the 1940s, Australia

1

has increasingly looked to another great empire for its security, the USA, which is why Australia has supported the USA in military actions in Vietnam, the Persian Gulf, Iraq and Afghanistan. In addition, for a time, I served in the Australian military and frequently worked beside military collegues from Singapore, the UK and the USA. I never served on active operations, but I took an oath of loyalty to the Queen and to the Australian people. At the same time, Australia is now economically closer to Asia than to Europe or North America. China is Australia's largest trading partner and India is now Australia's largest source of immigrants.

Why am I telling you this? Well, as you can see, the circumstances of my birth, the place where I grew up and the vocations I've had were directly related to the rise and fall of more than one empire. If there had been no German Reich, no Soviet Union and no British Empire, then perhaps I would never have been born, or at least never been born in Germany, never moved to Australia and never enlisted in the Army. I imagine that my life story is probably similar to that of many people. In fact, Tom Wright's father spent most of the Second World War as a prisoner of war, very fortunately surviving, even when many of his compatriots did not. Our lives have all been shaped by world empires in some way, by some previous conflict, by the prospect of future conflict or by the decisions of governments that are not our own. The history of the world has been about the clash of civilisations, the rise and fall of empires, great battles over political ideology, religious rivalry, East versus West, Marxism versus capitalism.

Except that the great clash of civilisations was supposed to be finished because the battle over ideologies was done and dusted. After the fall of the Berlin Wall (1989), the dissolution of the Soviet Union (1991), and the end of apartheid in South Africa (1994), it was clear to many that liberal democracy had won. Liberal democracy was *the system*, the climax and culmination of human political evolution. Liberal democracy was a social arrangement that balanced rights and responsibilities, freedom and order, centralised and distributed power, a system that could deliver sustainable economic growth. It was during the late 1980s that the American legal philosopher Francis Fukuyama wrote his celebrated *The End of History and the Last Man*, declaring in 1992 that:

> What we may be witnessing is not just the end of the Cold War, or the passing of a particular period of post-war history, but the end of history as such . . . That is, the end point of mankind's ideological evolution and the universalization of Western liberal democracy as the final form of human government.[1]

For a long time it looked as if Fukuyama was right. The world came together to defeat Saddam Hussein's Iraqi regime after it invaded Kuwait. Despite ethnic bloodshed in Rwanda and the former Yugoslavia, international intervention prevented further violence. Most countries were downsizing their militaries, the European Union was going from strength to strength, the internet was connecting people in whole new ways, and most economies were prospering in the 1990s. Western liberal democracy would now surely spread to Russia, China and the Middle East. 'History', conceived as the battle of ideas and clash of empires, had ended . . . or so we thought.

What came next in the final years of the twentieth century and in the first quarter of the twenty-first century were forces of chaos and cruelty that we thought had been vanquished for ever. There were drug cartels terrorising Latin America. There was the rise of radical Islam, September 11, 2001, and the global war on terror. These were followed by the Iraq War, the rise of Islamic State, civil war in Syria and a twenty-year occupation of Afghanistan ending with a calamitous retreat. The global financial crisis in 2008 strongly suggested that the whole economic system was a scam to make the filthy rich even richer. North Korea acquired nuclear weapons with Iran not far behind. China's economic rise did not lead to its democratic liberalisation; rather, the country turned into a wealthy and predatory superpower that runs a technological surveillance state. Despite hopes that Russia might become westernised, it seems that

---

1 Francis Fukuyama, *The End of History and the Last Man* (New York: Free Press, 1989), p. 4.

Russia remains what it has been ever since the seventeenth century: a military dictatorship. The Arab Spring rose and fell in a matter of a year. In the aftermath, none of the Arab states, except perhaps for Tunisia, is any freer than it was before. Added to that, the world is now experiencing the increasing effects of climate change, there are mass migrations of people fleeing conflict and poverty, and every nation remains ravaged by the effects of Covid-19. At the time of writing, Putin's Russia continues to devastate Ukraine, intent on either absorbing it or destroying it. China gazes menacingly upon Taiwan, persecutes religious minorities such as the Uighurs and Christian house churches, and ferociously cracks down on pro-democratic dissent in Hong Kong.

To add further insult to Fukuyama's thesis, the current state of many Western democracies is such that they are now fraught with fragmentation to the point of being caught in legislative deadlock or committed to some morbidly self-destructive feat of devouring themselves from the inside out. Places such as Australia and Italy have had a revolving door of prime ministers. Britain tore itself apart over Brexit. The USA convulses between its political extremes represented by white Christian nationalists and progressive identitarians. It lacks the consensus and belief in a greater good that once characterised its political class. The American political extremities believe that the other side should not even exist. America's respective news channels and social-media platforms attract viewers and rake in massive profits by pouring gasoline on the fires of grievance and stoking the embers of indifference. Then there are the lobbyists who buy politicians like someone collecting antique spoons. The West might not have hard corruption such as that found in a banana republic, but it is infested with the soft corruption of corporations that fund political campaigns to further their own interests. America's political actors and the tribalized media entities have based their funding models on hyping up audiences with the grievance *de jour*. The gambling industry has massive influence among the political class in the UK, Australia and Canada. It is sadly true that democratic parliaments and parties can be futile and insufferable in the same way as dictatorships are

4

brutal and intolerable.[2] This palpable democratic dysfunction gives China and Russia all the material they need for the claim of their own internal propaganda that democracy is a disordered and chaotic mess.

We are not the first ones to say so, but Fukuyama was wrong. History has not ended, empires are still on the march, and liberal democracy is not the bastion of benevolence that we like to pretend it is. Economic growth has not brought liberalism to China but rather drives its one-party authoritarianism. Russia has returned to its status quo as a military autocracy. Europe can't decide whether it wants to be the Habsburg Empire 2.0, a technocratic villain in a James Bond film, or a society of nationless nihilists where people are devoted to Europe in general but belong to nowhere in particular. The global war on terror peeled back the curtain to show that liberal democracies are heavily dependent on war for economic growth as well as for moral coherence.[3] The 2020s appear to be the most precarious and perilous time in human history since the 1930s. Except that, now, we have the additional nightmarish prospect of nuclear war, a catastrophic horror that is inevitable unless we make it impossible. There are parts of the world that could be set aflame by the smallest spark, such as an assassination, a company that goes bankrupt or a political coalition that falls apart. We have to contend with a deteriorating climate situation and further economic turmoil on the horizon. In addition, many liberal democracies find it impossible to reach any workable and equitable agreement on environmentalism, racial justice, healthcare, immigration, gun control, abortion, religious freedom and LGBTQ+ rights, leaving people with only fresh disgust at the system itself. The optimism of the early 1990s died on the killing fields of Kosovo, in the ruins of the World Trade Center and in the valleys of Afghanistan. Many commentators celebrated the demise of history. But, like a resurgent virus, history has struck back with a vengeance.

---

2 Jacques Ellul, *Anarchy and Christianity* (Grand Rapids, MI: Eerdmans, 1988), pp. 21–2.

3 On this, see Stanley Hauerwas and William H. Willimon, *Resident Aliens: Life in the Christian colony* (Nashville, TN: Abingdon, 1989), p. 35.

God's kingdom in a troubled world

A people of providence, purpose and prayer

In a world of rising empires, endless calamities, pandemics, terrorism, democratic disarray and culture wars, what is a Christian to think of all this, or to do about it?

The immediate thing that comes to mind is for us to consider God's *providence*. We know that whatever history is – cause and effect or clash of civilisations – God is ultimately sovereign over history. God is the God who 'deposes kings and sets up kings'[4] because 'dominion belongs to YHWH, / and he rules over the nations'.[5] Even amid the upheaval of nations, God dispenses in history and through history his common grace to all. God's goodness finds its way into our lives and homes despite the terror and trauma that ravages different regions of our world.

What is more, we do well to reflect on God's *purposes*. It is important to note that God does not program history like a computer programmer running an algorithm, but neither is God surprised by history. History is the theatre of divine glory, and all history will culminate in a dramatic moment when God puts the world to rights through Jesus.[6] History has an end date, and it's not when human beings upload their consciousness to artificial intelligence, when they set up a colony on Mars, or when our sun finally burns out. History itself is the canvas upon which God, in Jesus, answers and addresses the most pressing facets of human existence. The end of history is neither a whimper nor a bang, but creation itself transfigured into a new creation.[7]

In addition, the turmoil of our times means we must constantly be people of *prayer*. We have permission – and, indeed, a

---

4   Daniel 2:21.

5   Psalm 22:28.

6   N. T. Wright, *Surprised by Hope: Rethinking heaven, the resurrection and the mission of the Church* (London: SPCK, 2007), p. 152.

7   See N. T. Wright, *History and Eschatology: Jesus and the promise of natural theology* (Waco, TX: Baylor University Press, 2019).

command! – to pray, 'Rise up, O God, judge the earth, for all the nations belong to you!'[8] We should pray for our kings, prime ministers and presidents so that 'we may lead a tranquil and peaceful life, in all godliness and holiness'.[9] We can pray for peace, prosperity, justice and freedom as something to be enjoyed by peoples of every city, country and continent.

Building for the kingdom

Those points are all well and good, but we need more than things to console us and scriptural reflections for us to consider. In an age of ascending autocracies and dysfunctional democracies, the obvious question is: what should the Church do? We feel the urge, the itch, the need to do something, to act, not to stand idly by in an era of upheaval. Should we start our own political party, go to seminary to study for the ministry, join the marine corps or perhaps the peace corps, start a community garden, send more artillery to Ukraine, demand free healthcare, use the Black Lives Matter hashtag, march for religious freedom, donate to World Vision? Good questions for those who believe that we need to put our faith where our fear is and exercise a faith that works through love.[10]

We believe that the Church's answer to the global crises of our day is, in sum, the kingdom of God. The Church's message and mission rest on the notion that God is King, God has appointed Jesus as the King of kings and Lord of lords, and the Church's vocation is to build *for* the kingdom![11] Our working hypothesis is that the kingdom of God is not *from* this world, but it is emphatically *for* this world. The Church's kingdom-vocation is not only what it *says* to the world, but is also what the Church *does within and for* the sake of the world.[12]

---

8   Psalm 82:8.

9   1 Timothy 2:2. See also *1 Clement* 60.4 – 61.3; Polycarp, *Epistle to the Philippians* 12.3; Athenagoras, *Plea for the Christians* 37; Tertullian, *Apology* 30.4; 31.2; Origen, *Against Celsius* 8.73.

10   Revelation 2:10; Galatians 5:6.

11   Wright, *Surprised by Hope*, pp. 218–44.

12   Wright, *History and Eschatology*, p. 253.

We should note that the 'kingdom of God' can be defined in several ways, and we could explain it and break it down long into the night.[13] Suffice to say, the kingdom is about God's rescue and restoration of the entire creation as worked out in the context of Israel's covenantal history and God's action in the person and work of Jesus. In other words, God's kingdom is neither a timeless and abstract ideal nor the dissolution of the space–time universe. Rather, the kingdom of God refers to 'the action of the covenant God, within Israel's history, to restore her fortunes, to bring to an end the bitter period of exile, and to defeat, through her, the evil that ruled the whole world'.[14]

Jesus' message was that God was becoming king in and through his work, his preaching, his healings, and even by his death on the cross. Then, by his launching of the new creation in his resurrection and the gift of the spirit, the first followers of Jesus, taking their cue from their teacher, declared that the rebellious powers had been and were being defeated. Thereafter, creation was being healed and a new people, Jews and Gentiles together, were being redeemed and united in a renewed creation that could be anticipated by the gift of God's spirit. For the early church, the kingdom of God was never about going to heaven. It was a way of summarising what God had embryonically established in Jesus, the spirit-led work that God was doing among them in the present, and what God would establish in the fullness of time. It was this sense of God's kingdom, as something already anticipated, being carried forward, yet still hoped for, that defined the early church as a 'kingdom' movement.[15] Not a kingdom in the sense of an earthly empire or an ephemeral spiritual state, but as a vision and vocation for faithful action that works to bring God's kingship over every facet of human life.

---

13 See discussion in Michael F. Bird, *Evangelical Theology: A biblical and systematic introduction*, 2nd edn (Grand Rapids, MI: Zondervan, 2020), pp. 297–317; and Nicholas Perrin, *The Kingdom of God: A biblical theology* (Grand Rapids, MI: Zondervan, 2019).

14 N. T. Wright, *Jesus and the Victory of God*, Christian Origins and the Question of God 2 (London: SPCK, 1996), p. 307.

15 N. T. Wright, *The New Testament and the People of God*, Christian Origins and the Question of God 1 (London: SPCK, 1992), pp. 442, 459–64.

If we are to participate in and promote God's kingdom on earth, then we must refocus and redouble our efforts to enact this kingdom-project. The kingdom of God is the imperative that drives the Church's evangelistic preaching and its virtues, and compels us to reorder our lives according to the symbols and story of Jesus as the crucified, risen, and exalted king. But a caveat is needed lest we naively equate our own efforts directly with the kingdom of God itself. That is why, as we have already said (echoing Paul in Colossians 4:11), we have spoken not of 'building the kingdom' but of building for the kingdom.

We act in faith, hope and love in the present, offering our lives as a living sacrifice to our exalted Lord. Then, in the power of the spirit, we prepare this sin-cursed and war-torn earth to receive the reign of God on the day when heaven and earth are married together. We really do want, as best as we can, to make God's kingdom 'come' so that it may be 'on earth as it is in heaven'.[16] We are, by our kingdom-labours, preparing the bride to meet the groom, setting the table for the wedding supper of the Lamb, and curating creation for the day when God will be 'all in all'.[17]

But here's the question for us today, the one that we intend to explore in this book. How do we build for the kingdom of God amid Afghan and Ukrainian refugees in France? How do we build for the kingdom while seeing the injustices that afflict people of colour and indigenous peoples in the West? How do we build for the kingdom in a seminary in Taiwan under the shadow of Chinese aggression? How do we build for the kingdom while reckoning with the past and present evils of our own democratic institutions? How do we build for the kingdom with our own divided politics over abortion and climate change? Are we more shaped by social media than Scripture? And, most challenging of all, how do we build for the kingdom in the face of menacing empires while resisting the inevitable seduction to create an empire of our own? Such things call for wisdom and discernment.

---

16 Cf. Matthew 6:10.
17 1 Corinthians 15:28.

Hard as those questions are, we need more than ever to recover our kingdom-vocation. For our days are mired in one tragedy after another, truth has become tribalised, despots seem undefeatable, democracies appear endemically defective, and masses of men and women have dulled their senses into moral apathy by giving themselves over to the mind-numbing frivolity of their i-devices. To build for the kingdom we need to confront the difficult subject of empire, appreciate the ambiguous place that Christianity has occupied in Western civilisation, and consider how best to offer a Christian witness in an age that has lost its ability to reason with others.

Why do the nations rage against YHWH and his anointed?

Let us begin with Hong Kong theologian Kwok Pui-Lan on the importance of empire for the study of Christianity:

> Christianity cannot be understood apart from empire. We cannot understand the Bible without knowing something about the struggles for survival of the Hebrew people under the Babylonian, Assyrian, Persian, Greek, and Roman Empires. Christianity began in the Roman Empire, in which Jesus and the early disciples lived as colonised peoples. Jesus died on the cross, which was a symbol of state terrorism and a form of torture and punishment for political rebels.[18]

The Bible is a book utterly immersed in empire. Its stories are set in the midst of the great empires of Egypt, Assyria, Babylon, Persia, Macedonia, the Ptolemies and Seleucids, and then finally the Roman Empire. The Israelites were often caught between and conquered by these great empires. Yes, there were brief periods of independence and even expansion, first under King Solomon, then much later by the Hasmoneans. But the Israelites most of the time

---

18 Kwok Pui-Lan, *Postcolonial Politics and Theology: Unraveling empire for a global world* (Philadelphia, PA: Westminster John Knox, 2021), p. 77.

were either living under the shadow of empire or experiencing the terror of empire. They were either vassals or victims of the imperial powers that towered over them. Yet that is not the whole story. The testimony of Scripture is that kings and empires are raised up and brought down as Israel's God so pleases.

God raised up Pharoah to show his power and to make his name resound throughout all the earth by delivering the Hebrews from Egypt, the house of slavery.[19] Psalm 2 celebrates the enthronement of Israel's new Davidic king, a divine son, appointed to rule the nations as YHWH's representative on earth. The nations of the world may howl in rage and rancour against YHWH and his anointed. But YHWH looks down upon them and laughs, for their rebellion is as futile as it is foolish. YHWH and his anointed 'son' break the arrogance of empires.[20]

The problem was that it did not always work out that way. Israel's vocation, given to them by YHWH, was to be a kingdom of priests and a light to the nations. Tragically, though, the Israelites often violated their covenantal task when they imitated the idolatrous evils of the nations around them, and so received the curses of the covenant to which they were bonded. Such curses included foreign domination, exile and desolation. Yet even that was not the end of the story: God's mercy was always greater than their wayward disobedience.

In the eighth century BC, the ten northern tribes of Israel were taken into exile by the Assyrian King Sennacherib, with the two southern tribes of Judah and Benjamin only narrowly escaping the Assyrian onslaught. Sadly, almost two centuries later, the southern kingdom would suffer the same fate with its inhabitants violently taken into exile by King Nebuchadnezzar of Babylon. The prophet Jeremiah, who had warned his contemporaries of what was going to happen, wept for Jerusalem and the destruction of its temple by the Babylonians.[21] Recalling the national disaster, the Psalter lamented the dishevelled survivors, hollowed out by hunger, being ordered by their captors to 'sing us one of the songs of

---

19 Exodus 9:16; 20:2.
20 Psalm 2:1–11.
21 Jeremiah 9.

Zion' as they sat beside the banks of the Euphrates.[22] How could they sing? All they could do was weep!

It was at this time that Habakkuk cried out, 'O YHWH, how long...?' as the Babylonian hordes unleashed their campaign of destruction upon Judah.[23] God's answer to Habakkuk was that 'there is still a vision for the appointed time; it speaks of the end and does not lie. If it seems to tarry, wait for it; it will surely come; it will not delay. Look at the proud! Their spirit is not right in them, but the righteous live by their faithfulness.'[24] In other words, Babylon's power was not unbreakable, its victories not final; a day of recompense was indeed coming. Until then, the people needed to keep faith in God's own faithfulness to them. In response, Habakkuk goes away rejoicing 'in the God of my salvation'.[25] Habakkuk understood how empires made history, a history made of desolation wrought by kings who believed they were walking and talking icons of their own deities. Yet the God of the covenant, while he might use these kings for his own purposes, would never let them have it all their own way. That is precisely why the Welsh preacher Martyn Lloyd-Jones said that these three short chapters of the book of Habakkuk provide God's answer to the 'problem of history'.[26]

Isaiah has much to say about God's kingship and the promise of Israel's rescue and restoration from captivity in Babylon. A particularly powerful moment comes in Isaiah 52 where there is a royal proclamation of glad tidings that YHWH is going to show the true extent of his kingly power and lordship over history:

> Awake; awake;
>   put on your strength, O Zion!
> Put on your beautiful garments,
>   O Jerusalem, the holy city,

---

22 Psalm 137:3–4.

23 Habakkuk 1:2.

24 Habakkuk 2:3–4.

25 Habakkuk 3:18.

26 Martyn Lloyd-Jones, *From Fear to Faith: Studies in the book of Habakkuk and the problem of history* (London: Inter-Varsity Press, 1953).

for the uncircumcised and the unclean
    shall enter you no more.
Shake yourself from the dust; rise up,
    O captive Jerusalem;
loose the bonds from your neck,
    O captive daughter Zion!

For thus says YHWH: You were sold for nothing, and you shall be redeemed without money. For thus says the Lord GOD: Long ago, my people went down into Egypt to reside there as aliens; the Assyrian, too, has oppressed them without cause. Now therefore what am I doing here, says YHWH, seeing that my people are taken away without cause? Their rulers howl, says YHWH, and continually, all day long, my name is despised. Therefore my people shall know my name; on that day they shall know that it is I who speak – it is I!

How beautiful upon the mountains are the feet of
    the messenger who announces peace,
who brings good news, who announces salvation,
    who says to Zion, 'Your God reigns.'
Listen! Your sentinels lift up their voices; together
    they shout for joy,
for in plain sight they see the return of YHWH to Zion.
Break forth; shout together for joy, you ruins of
    Jerusalem,
for YHWH has comforted his people; he has
    redeemed Jerusalem.
YHWH has bared his holy arm before the eyes of
    all the nations,
and all the ends of the earth shall see the
    salvation of our God.
(Isaiah 52:1–10, amended)

The messenger declares the demise of Babylon and the liberation of enslaved Israel, summed up with two Hebrew words, *malak elohayik*, 'Your God reigns.'[27] In other words, God has become King; God has overthrown the tyrant, not merely a Near Eastern despot, but the dark spiritual forces that stand behind him. This was proof of God's covenant faithfulness and God's sovereignty over the nations.[28] God did that by raising up another king, Cyrus of the Persian Empire, to subdue the Babylonians and strip them of their power; and then appointed him to rebuild Jerusalem and set captive Israel free.[29] This is also the context in which we are to understand the suffering 'Servant' of Isaiah 53. The Servant's affliction and vindication is a microcosm of the story of Israel, suffering at the hands of pagan oppressors, but trusting in God to put things right in the final assize. A passage of Scripture that was to be very important for the early church.

Turning to the book of Daniel, we have a mixture of court tales and apocalyptic visions that show God's providence over the rise and fall of empires and God's preservation of his people even within the apparatus of empire. Quite noticeably, the conflict between Israel's God and the pagan empires becomes incredibly acute. The climax of that confrontation arrives in Daniel 7, with the vision of the four beasts, representing the kingdoms of Babylon, Medo-Persia, Macedon and the Seleucids – or some variation thereof.[30] Then the scene suddenly changes to the heavenly throne-room where the Ancient of Days takes his throne with myriads of angelic attendants. It is there that we are introduced to a mysterious human-like figure, who is the divine answer to the earthly monsters that dominate the earth and devour the flesh of God's people:

As I watched in the night visions,

I saw one like a human being
    coming with the clouds of heaven.

---

27 Isaiah 52:7.

28 N. T. Wright, *How God Became King: Getting to the heart of the Gospels* (London: SPCK, 2012), p. 181.

29 Isaiah 45:1–2, 12–13 See also 2 Chr. 36:22–23.

30 Daniel 7:1–8.

And he came to the Ancient One
    and was presented before him.
To him was given dominion
    and glory and kingship,
that all peoples, nations, and languages
    should serve him.
His dominion is an everlasting dominion
    that shall not pass away,
and his kingship is one
    that shall never be destroyed.
(Daniel 7:13–14)

The 'one like a son of man' has excited interpretations as to whether he is an angelic creature or a messianic agent. Most likely, the man is a multivalent symbol who represents God's kingship, God's anointed king and God's royal people. The man is the heavenly embodiment of God's earthly people and the divine counterpart to the arrogant horn who speaks in arrogant tones.[31] The vision, then, is about the exaltation and vindication of God's people in God's appointed human agent, who will one day rise and reign over the idolatrous and inhumane powers in the coming age. It was a vision that was to have a monumental impact upon Jewish authors, the historical Jesus, the Evangelists and John of Patmos.

Kings and empires may 'rage' and 'conspire' against God and his anointed king, but they are doomed to failure.[32] They are like ants building a rampart against a lion. From Isaiah, we hear that the king of Babylon might think of himself as an ascending star, destined to rise above and reign beyond the celestial bodies, unaware that God intends to bring him down to the pit of death to be left as carrion for scavengers.[33] Though a succession of empires rises one after another, Daniel tells us that 'the God of heaven will set up a kingdom that shall never be destroyed, nor shall this kingdom be

---

31 Daniel 7:8. We think the arrogant horn is the Seleucid king Antiochus Epiphanes IV who, a Jewish epitomist said, thought himself 'equal to God' (2 Maccabees 9:12).

32 Psalm 2:1; Acts 4:25–6; Revelation 11:18.

33 Isaiah 14:3–21.

left to another people. It shall crush all these kingdoms and bring them to an end, and it shall stand for ever.' It is this kingdom that will be like 'a stone', hurled at the clay feet of earthly rulers, until they acclaim that Israel's 'God is God of gods and Lord of kings'.[34] Kings who announce their unrivalled power and attire themselves as living deities might terrorise God's people and taunt them with great boasts of their supremacy. But they themselves are servants of the Most High, not the invincible and inviolable semi-divine beings they might think they are, and they can be brought down just as quickly as they were raised up.

The arrogance of empires and their despotic kings reminds us of Percy Bysshe Shelley's famous poem 'Ozymandias'. In the poem, a man hears from a traveller about the ruined statue of King Ozymandias, who once ruled a vast and mighty kingdom, which now lies in ruins mostly buried beneath desert dunes. The statue of King Ozymandias is partly smashed, half sunk in sand, and his once great kingdom is laid waste. All that is left of it now is the 'shattered visage' of its ruler. Upon the crumbling monument is an inscription of Ozymandias to his own greatness: 'My name is Ozymandias, king of kings: / Look on my works, ye Mighty, and despair!' King Ozymandias, like the potentates of all empires, made outlandish boasts of his magnificence, his invincibility and his terror to his vassals. Yet now his self-aggrandising monument is nothing more than debris. Ozymandias is remembered, but not for glory or for greatness, only for the depths of his arrogance.

God has written on the walls of palaces and on the tapestry of history that every empire that sets itself up against him will be weighed, measured and found wanting.[35] For the day is drawing inevitably nearer when 'the kingdom of the world has passed to our Lord and his Messiah . . . and he will reign forever and ever'.[36]

---

34 Daniel 2:44–7.
35 Daniel 5:1–31.
36 Revelation 11:15.

Jesus, the early church and the Roman Empire

When we get to the first century, Rome had become the dominant military empire of the Mediterranean. Rome had seen off its Carthaginian rivals in north Africa, and then gradually devoured one territory after another, until its empire extended from Spain to Syria, from the Danube to the Nile. The Roman Empire was, as empires have tended to be, built on a system of plunder, enslavement and exploitation. Most Roman history was written by Roman elite men detailing the accomplishments of themselves and their peers. But every now and then, one finds a slight hint of protest at the cruelties imposed on the many subjugated tribes. The historian Tacitus puts into the mouth of the Pictish king Calgacus words that describe the Romans as a rapacious and predacious people:

> They ransack the world, and now that the earth fails to contain their all-devastating grasp, they scour even the sea: if their enemy has wealth, they are greedy; if he is poor, they are ambitious; neither East nor West has satiated their hunger . . . They plunder, they murder, they rape, all in the name of their so-called empire. And where they have left desolation, they call it 'peace'.[37]

The great Roman peace was a peace that was created and sustained by merciless violence.

Furthermore, the Roman Empire transformed itself from a republic into an autocracy. After a series of destabilising civil wars, the man who finally emerged triumphant was Octavius Caesar. Octavius had defeated the senatorial cabal who murdered his adopted father Julius Caesar, and he then crushed his former ally turned arch-rival Mark Antony. Thereafter, Octavius reached a point of unrivalled supremacy and yet, ever the statesman, he knew that he had to try to keep up the appearance that Rome was still a

---

37 Tacitus, *Agricola* 30, translation mine (M. Bird).

17

republic. So Octavius merely made himself *princeps,* 'first-citizen', rather than a king or dictator. The Roman senate wisely accepted his arrangement – as if they had a choice – and concurred that Octavius would govern the more vulnerable (and valuable!) provinces such as Spain, Gaul, Egypt and Syria while they attended to the domestic front and less volatile regions. Still, the Roman elites rushed to honour him with consulships, enrolled him in priesthoods, held festivals in his honour, and bestowed honourific titles upon him such as 'Augustus' (venerable one). Concurrently, in the East, there was a mad dash by former clients of Mark Antony to ingratiate themselves to this new regime by building temples to Octavius and offering him divine honours. Even the Judaean monarch Herod the Great, a former loyal supporter of Antony, joined in, erecting lavish temples to Octavius in nearby Gentile cities such as Caesarea to ingratiate himself with his new Roman master. Herod was trying to keep the balance between demonstrating his imperial allegiance and doing anything that might enrage his fiercely monotheistic Jewish subjects.

Jesus grew up in the Galilean village of Nazareth only a few miles south of the province's leading city of Sepphoris. After the death of Herod the Great in 4 BC, a figure known as Judas ben Hezekiah led a popular uprising against the Herodian regime. He captured Sepphoris and quickly seized the armoury. In direct response, Varus, the Roman legate of Syria, arrived with his legions and auxiliaries and crushed the uprising, sacking Sepphoris, and selling the inhabitants into slavery.[38] Ten years later in AD 6, when Herod's son Archelaus was dismissed from his post as ethnarch, Jewish territories reverted to direct Roman rule. After a census was announced – and a census was always for the purpose of taxation – Judas the Galilean and his followers launched another revolt in Galilee, to throw off the shackles of Roman taxation, on the premise that the Jews had no king but God. But once again, the rebellion was brutally repressed.[39] Jesus thus grew up in the immediate

---

38 Josephus, *Ant.* 17.271–2, 286–98; *War* 2.55–6, 66–79.
39 Josephus, *Ant.* 18.23–5; *War* 2.118, 433; Acts 5:37.

aftermath of the failed Galilean rebellions where the physical signs and traumatic memories of Roman imperial violence, including crucifixions, were everywhere. Roman armies had swept through the region and brought with them bloodshed, destruction, murder, rape, plundering and enslavement.[40] That is the context in which Jesus soon began his ministry proclaiming the kingdom of God.

Thus, when Jesus proclaimed that 'The time is fulfilled! . . . God's kingdom is arriving! Turn back, and believe the good news!'[41] he wasn't offering people four spiritual laws or a road to heavenly bliss. Rather, Jesus was saying that the prophetic promises about the end of exile, a new exodus, a new covenant, a new temple, Israel's regathering and restoration, were at last coming true. God was coming and coming as king. The kingship of God was being manifested through the things Jesus himself was doing: his own mighty deeds, healings, exorcisms and even his death.[42] The day was coming, and was now already here, when the empires of this age would be eclipsed and judged by the kingly power of Israel's God.

The apostle Paul set forth a scheme whereby the kingdom was envisaged as a two-act drama. First, there was God's royal rescuing power, executed in Jesus' messianic mission, his crucifixion 'for our sins', his resurrection as the 'firstborn from among the dead', and experienced in the giving of the holy spirit.[43] Second, there was to be a future reckoning: 'Then comes the end, the goal, when he [i.e. Jesus] hands over the kingly rule to God the father, when he has destroyed all rule and all authority and power.'[44] But what did Jesus' exaltation to the Father's right hand and the prophecy of Jesus' return mean for Caesar?[45]

---

40 Josephus, *Ant.* 17.285–91; *War* 2.68–71.

41 Mark 1:15.

42 See Matthew 12:28/Luke 11:20; Matthew 11:5/Luke 7:22–3; Mark 9:1.

43 See Romans 5:18–19; 8:29; 15:8; 1 Corinthians 15:3, 20; 2 Corinthians 5:5; Ephesians 1:13; Colossians 1:18.

44 1 Corinthians 15:24.

45 For our thoughts on Paul and the Roman Empire, see N. T. Wright, *Paul and the Faithfulness of God*, Christian Origins and the Question of God 4 (London: SPCK, 2013), pp. 1271–1319; and Michael F. Bird, *An Anomalous Jew: Paul among Jews, Greeks, and Romans* (Grand Rapids, MI: Eerdmans, 2016), pp. 205–55.

The Romans knew of Jewish messianic hopes and sneered at them with abject contempt. Regarding the Judaean rebellion of AD 66–70, Tacitus said:

> Some few put a fearful meaning on these events, but in most there was a firm persuasion, that in the ancient records of their priests was contained a prediction of how at this very time the East was to grow powerful, and rulers, coming from Judaea, were to acquire universal empire.[46]

Suetonius similarly declared:

> There had spread over all the Orient an old and established belief, that it was fated at that time for men coming from Judaea to rule the world.[47]

The problem was that in Paul's day, Nero Caesar was lauded as 'Lord of the entire world',[48] and he and his regime had no intention of indulging, from their perspective, wild fantasies of liberation won by the Judaeans and their tribal deity. In the mind of Roman elites, the gods had decreed that the Romans had been ordained as masters of the West and East, sent to bring peace and security to the barbarous tribes of the inhabited world. The poetry of Horace and Virgil is saturated with lines and language about how the Romans were the divinely appointed masters of the world.

One only needs to read Paul's call for submission to earthly authorities in Romans 13:1–7 to know that he was not planning a palace coup to replace Nero with the nearest senator who would make Christianity legal or even promote it to a privileged position within the empire. Be that as it may, Paul's gospel, centred as it was on the proclamation that 'Jesus is Lord', had sociopolitical

---

46 Tacitus, *Histories* 5.13.
47 Suetonius, *Vespasian* 4.4.
48 *Sylloge Inscriptionum Graecarum* 814.30–1 (AD 67), cited in Joseph D. Fantin, *The Lord of the Entire World: Lord Jesus, a challenge to Lord Caesar?* (Sheffield: Sheffield Phoenix Press, 2011), p. 199.

implications. Paul's mind, which was rooted in Scripture and set aflame by his encounter with the risen Jesus, was resolute in the belief that the world rightfully belonged, not to the son of Augustus, but to the Son of David. No wonder then that Paul deploys Isaiah's language to declare that Jesus is 'the one who rises up to rule the nations; the nations shall hope in him'.[49] Paul's kingdom-charged gospel was embedded in the Jewish tradition of YHWH's contest against the powers and pantheon of the pagan world. To declare that Jesus is Lord was to imply that Caesar is not.[50]

Even to whisper 'Jesus is Lord', then, carried with it an air of challenge, that perhaps Caesar's lordship, with its pretention to divine status and unrivalled supremacy, spoke not to invincibility but to idolatry. This is precisely why the pagan philosopher Celsius accused the Christians of being guilty of 'religious rantings' or 'seditious sayings' by devoting themselves exclusively to Jesus and refusing to honour local and imperial deities.[51] If so, then, it means that Paul was not a travelling evangelist offering people a new religious experience, but an ambassador for a king-in-waiting, establishing cells of people loyal to this new king, and ordering their lives according to his story, his symbols and his praxis, and their minds according to his truth. This could only be construed as deeply counter-imperial, as subversive to the whole edifice of the Roman Empire; and there is in fact plenty of evidence that Paul intended it to be so construed, and that when he ended up in prison as a result of his work he took it as a sign that he had been doing his job properly.[52]

---

49 Romans 15:12 from Isaiah 11:10.

50 N. T. Wright, *Paul in Fresh Perspective* (Minneapolis, MN: Fortress, 2009), p. 69.

51 Origen, *Against Celsius* 8.2. Martin Hengel quotes Karlmann Beyschlag that 'Celsius was, as far as we can tell, the first to attribute to Christianity, in a negative sense to be sure, a pronounced "theology of revolution"'. See *Christ and Power* (Philadelphia, PA: Fortress, 1977), p. 41.

52 N. T. Wright, 'Paul's Gospel and Caesar's Empire', in *Paul and Politics: Ekklesia, Israel, imperium, interpretation: Essays in honour of Krister Stendahl*, ed. R. H. Horsley (Harrisburg, PA: Trinity Press International, 2000), pp. 161–2. Reprinted in N. T. Wright, *Pauline Perspectives: Essays on Paul, 1978–2013* (London: SPCK, 2013), ch. 12.

John's apocalypse is a book of strange and powerful images.[53] It contains epistles that exhort and admonish the churches of Roman Asia. It is a prophecy of things now foretold yet still to come. Its visions are pervaded by scriptural imagery, packed densely with intricate symbolism, providing an unveiling of how things in heaven mirror things on earth. This book is not intended to be an apocalyptic soap opera; rather, it is a socio-religious critique of Roman power and propaganda. John's apocalypse is unique because, unlike most literature of the time, it shows us what the Roman Empire looked like from the perspective of those with the boot of Roman power upon their throat. This is why there is so much attention given to the 'beast' (i.e. the Roman Empire) and the false prophet (i.e. the imperial cult and the worship of the emperor). We should not treat the book as an esoteric and encoded forecast of historical events about ourselves but as a theocentric vision of the coming of God's universal kingdom that spoke powerfully and prophetically to the churches of Asia Minor. John was calling on his fellow believers to see what he saw, that Roman power, for all its self-vaunted greatness and glory, was a predatory and idolatrous fusion of greed, arrogance and violence that was ripe for judgement like grapes ready for harvest. Rome would be judged, Rome would fall, as would all empires that set themselves up against the Lord God and his Messiah.

The end of empires

The early church inherited the anti-pagan and anti-imperial perspective of its Jewish heritage.[54] The kingship of God, and his Messiah, was set up against the empires of the world. Jesus was crucified by a second-tier Roman official in a backwater province,

---

53 See N. T. Wright and Michael F. Bird, *The New Testament in Its World: An introduction to the history, literature, and theology of the first Christians* (Grand Rapids, MI: Zondervan, 2019), pp. 808–48.

54 A point first noted by the pagan philosopher Celsius (Origen, *Against Celsus*, 3.5–10).

killed like a lowly slave, brutally executed like a murderous brigand. But God had raised Jesus from the dead, undoing what Pilate and Herod had done to him, robbing death of its finality, and testifying to the goodness of God's power and the power of God's goodness. Death was the tyrant's ultimate weapon to terrify and enslave, yet God's power and promise of resurrection meant that the tyrant's weapon had been disarmed.[55] Beyond that, God the Father had appointed Jesus as the Son of God in power, Messiah and Lord, and Jesus would return to judge the world with true justice. One day, empires as the world has known them will be no more.

Well before the final judgement, still within the annals of history, a moment was soon to come when a Roman Caesar, Emperor Constantine, would order his soldiers to put the sign of the cross on their shields. An act that marked the end of the cross as a symbol of Roman tyranny over Christians and marked instead the beginning of a new era when Rome would see herself as a faithful servant of the Lord Jesus Christ. As Will Durant famously said:

> There is no greater drama in human record than the sight of a few Christians, scorned or oppressed by a succession of emperors, bearing all trials with a fierce tenacity, multiplying quietly, building order while their enemies generated chaos, fighting the sword with the word, brutality with hope, and at last defeating the strongest state that history has known. Caesar and Christ had met in the arena, and Christ had won.[56]

In AD 300 about 10% of the Roman Empire was Christian. By 380, however, 50% of the population were Christian, including emperors, generals and governors of the realm. Christianity was not only legalised but also quickly became the main religious force within the empire, eclipsing hundreds of years of pagan religion.

---

55 N. T. Wright, *The Resurrection of the Son of God*, Christian Origins and the Question of God 3 (London: SPCK, 2003), p. 730.

56 Will Durant, *The Story of Civilisation: Caesar and Christ* (New York: Simon & Schuster, 1944), p. 652.

The blood of the Lamb was indeed victorious over the soldiers and swords of Caesar and his minions. While that is the end of one story, it is also the beginning of another one. Thereafter the Church had to shift from resisting empire to residing within the empire as a privileged guest. A situation that was filled with its own problems and complications.

2

The Church between Jesus and Caesar

How the Church revolutionised the Roman Empire

The early church had to negotiate empire, resist empire, flee from the empire, suffer under the empire, offer apologies for itself to the empire . . . until the Church became one with the empire. A fateful moment of transition. Over the first three centuries, Christians were sometimes begrudgingly tolerated, but at other times they were the victims of local and even empire-wide persecutions. The Roman persecution of Christianity as a seditious misanthropic cult ended with the conversion of Constantine and his subsequent patronage of the Christian religion. Constantine's victory over Maxentius at the Milvian Bridge just outside Rome in AD 312 made him the supreme Roman ruler of the West. Constantine attributed that victory to the providence of the one true God and the power of Jesus Christ. That was immediately followed by the end of persecutions and the gradual adoption of Christianity as the official state religion in the coming decades. As many had foreseen, Caesar had at last bowed his knee before Christ.

In less than ten years, from the brutal Diocletian persecutions in AD 303, to the Edict of Milan in 313 granting Christians official legal protections, the fate of Christians at the hands of the Roman Empire had radically shifted from utter hopelessness to blessed reprieve. In an even more dramatic shift, Christianity would move from being merely tolerated to becoming hegemonic. How did followers of

Jesus fare in this new arrangement, finding themselves no longer martyrs but chaplains to the empire? Under Roman sponsorship, Christians were no longer hunted, but were now able to hound and harass their traditional rivals among pagans, Jews and heretical Christian sects. Indeed, Christianity, through its bishops, became a powerful player in the halls of imperial power, in both Rome and Constantinople. At its worst, the Church then became an instrument of empire, offering Christ's insignia to the decrees of soldier-emperors who continued to do what empires always do: conquer, enslave and exploit. The Church came to exchange the cross of Christ for the sword of Rome.

That said, for all the evils of Christendom, with its marriage of Church and State, with the duumvirate of bishop and king, there were genuinely positive and ultimately revolutionary changes for human civilisation. Over the centuries, the Latin West and the Greek East became increasingly shaped by a Christian vision of God's love for the world and the place of Christian virtues in societies where few restraints on evil and exploitation existed. Consider this: once upon a time, the pagan philosopher Celsius could look down upon Christianity as a detestable and servile religion that only attracted 'the foolish, the dishonourable, and stupid, only women, slaves, and little children'. Christianity to Celsius was unmanly and un-Roman because at its centre was a so-called crucified god, adored and worshipped by the feeble-minded and weak-bodied dregs of society.[1] Celsius was typical of Roman aversion to the cult of the crucified Nazarene. Beginning with Constantine's legislation and empowerment of clergy, Christianity began a social, legal and moral revolution that still echoes today. Political philosopher Nassim Nicholas Taleb captures just how radical the Christian message was in a world where the gods were powers and power was worshipped:

The Greco-Romans despised the feeble, the poor, the sick, and the disabled; Christianity glorified the weak, the downtrodden, and the untouchable; and does that all the way

[1] Origen, *Against Celsius* 3.44.

to the top of the pecking order. While ancient gods could have their share of travails and difficulties, they remained in that special class of gods. But Jesus was the first ancient deity who suffered the punishment of the slave, the lowest ranking member of the human race. And the sect that succeeded him generalized such glorification of suffering: dying as an inferior is more magnificent than living as the mighty. The Romans were befuddled to see members of that sect use for symbol the cross – the punishment for slaves. It had to be some type of joke in their eyes.[2]

The Christians turned the whole edifice of gods, power, greatness and hierarchy on its head. God had used the foolish to shame the wise. God was a defender of the poor and champion of the weak. The rich would be sent away hungry while the poor would be well fed. A time was coming when there would be a reordering of power: the first would be last and the last would be first. So the rich had to mourn and wail for their riches lest these become evidence against them at the final judgement. Christians were accused of 'turning the world upside down'[3] and it would seem in that task that they were wholly successful because we live in a world where the weak and victimised are given almost sacral status.

Many so-called intellectuals keep pushing the tiresome notion that Christianity engineered the Dark Ages to stifle learning, to sponsor the divine right of kings, and to build religious capital into the walls of oppression. Further, they often spout the view that every advancement of human rights and every progression of human endeavour derives from intellectual seeds sown by the French Revolution and from the freethinkers of the Enlightenment. Sceptics even have the gall to claim that the rise of modern science and the abolition of slavery all happened in spite of Christianity, not

2   Nassim Nicholas Taleb, 'On Christianity: An essay as a foreword for Tom Holland's *Dominion*', *Incerto*, 26 August 2022: https://medium.com/incerto/on-christianity-b7fecde866ec (accessed 14 August 2023).

3   Acts 17:6.

because of it.[4] Yet that old chestnut, well-worn as it is, has one fatal flaw: it is not true.[5]

Most people in today's world recognise as noble the ideas that we should love our enemies, that the strong should protect the weak, and that it is better to suffer evil than to do evil. People in the West treat such things as self-evident moral facts. Yet such values were certainly not self-evident to the Greeks, Romans, Arabs, Vikings, Ottomans, Mongols or Aztecs. The reason why most people today accept those ideals as axiomatic is that we are products of the Christian revolution. Even when people hotly deny this, insisting (with some justification) that it's the Church that has been 'the oppressor', the moral protest against oppression is itself rooted in Christian belief. For the Christian message is that all human beings reflect the image of God: God loved the world so much that he sent his Son to save it, and the cross proves that true power is found in weakness, greatness is attained in service, revenge only begets greater evil, and all victims will be vindicated at God's judgement seat. That is what has been wired into the moral compass of Western civilisation. Whether we are conservatives who believe that voiceless and vulnerable babies should not have their lives ripped apart in utero, or progressives who contend that women have the right to have control over their own bodies, we are all arguing in Christian language, and we are all trading in Christian currency.

To unpack that thesis further, we should note that the Apostle Paul did not march around the Roman Forum with a sign saying, 'Slave lives matter!' Yet the words he wrote in Galatians 3:28, that in the Messiah, 'there is no longer slave or free; there is no "male and female"', laid the bedrock for the abolition of slavery and the founding of feminism. For the Romans, every master had the right to the sexual 'use' of his wife and slaves, to do with their bodies as he saw fit. Horace, a Roman poet of the Augustan Age, once mused, 'When your organ is stiff, and a servant girl or a young boy from the

---

4   A view propounded by the eighteenth-century Roman historian Edward Gibbon and even by contemporary cognitive scientist Steven Pinker today.

5   Here we are indebted to Tom Holland, *Dominion: How the Christian revolution remade the world* (New York: Basic, 2019), esp. pp. 80–106.

household is near at hand and you know you can make an immediate assault, would you sooner burst with tension? Not me: I like
sex to be there and easy to get.'[6] In sharp contrast to Horace, Paul
warned the Thessalonians against pursuing their unbridled lusts
and of the dire judgement awaiting those who exploited others:

> For this is the will of God, your sanctification: that you abstain
> from sexual immorality; that each one of you know how to
> control your own body in holiness and honour, not with lustful
> passion, like the gentiles who do not know God; that no one
> wrong or exploit a brother or sister in this matter, because the
> Lord is an avenger in all these things, just as we have already
> told you beforehand and solemnly warned you.[7]

Paul too requested that a slave-owner named Philemon welcome
back an absconded slave named Onesimus, not begrudgingly or
with a view to a beating, but as 'a beloved brother'.[8] Paul told the
men of Corinth that 'the man isn't in charge of his own body; his
wife is'[9] and he prohibited the Ephesian men from working as 'slave
traders'.[10] To us, we read that and think, 'Well, obviously!' But the
first recipients who heard these words probably blinked or gaped
with astonishment and uttered the words, 'Is he joking?'

To give another example, Luke the Evangelist summarised Paul's
speech on the Athenian Areopagus, telling the philosophically
savvy civic leaders there that all humanity shared a common
ancestry, that God 'hath made of one blood all nations of men for
to dwell on all the face of the earth'.[11] Those words 'of one blood'
seem innocent to us, but this was the verse beyond all others that
was preached, printed, yelled and cried by abolitionists, African

---

6 Horace, *Satires* 1.2.116–19 (trans. N. Rudd).

7 1 Thessalonians 4:3–6 (NRSVue).

8 Philemon 16.

9 1 Corinthians 7:4.

10 1 Timothy 1:10.

11 Acts 17:26 (KJV). The Greek word for 'blood' is in fact missing from most good early
manuscripts of the NT, but the point Paul is making is the same.

American clergy, and advocates for indigenous communities to demand justice for people of colour against oppression by white slave-holders and mistreatment by colonial masters.[12] It was such words that led Hannah More to write her 1788 poem 'Slavery': 'Shall Britain, where the soul of Freedom reigns, / Forge chains for others she herself disdains?'[13]

Sceptics not yet convinced of the thesis that Christianity has shaped Western values more than anything might want to consider one more example. The Roman emperor Claudius celebrated his conquest of Britain by commissioning a marble relief for the Sebasteion of Aphrodisias in Caria which depicted him, muscular and mighty, dominating and raping a female captive of Britain.[14] We gasp with horror at such a thing. We find it hideously evil and morally affronting. Who would celebrate a military victory today with a monument depicting their head of state committing an act of sexual violence and murder? Why is our outrage at Claudius's marble relief a natural reflex? Why do we think to raise up the victims of violence? It is because, whether we like it or not, no matter how irreligious we may claim to be, we have all internalised our own Christian revolution. We believe, almost by instinct, that things ought to be 'on earth as in heaven'. Christendom might be no more politically, but it still casts a long beam of light over the moral vision of Western societies. The Christian Scriptures scripted the social and sexual revolutions of the modern age.

The Church's unholy alliance with the Roman Empire

It is fair to say that the creation of a Christian political order was never the Church's purpose. The political order that became Christendom was simply the result of the success of the Church's

---

12 See John W. Harris, *One Blood: 200 years of Aboriginal encounter with Christianity: A story of hope* (Sutherland: Albatross, 1994); Lisa M. Bowens, *African American Readings of Paul: Reception, resistance, and transformation* (Grand Rapids, MI: Eerdmans, 2020).

13 Cited in Luke Bretherton, *Christ and the Common Life: Political theology and the case for democracy* (Grand Rapids, MI: Eerdmans, 2019), p. 189.

14 See https://preview.redd.it/54odxcdqoeu51.jpg?auto=webp&v=enabled&s=69c0519d1db03 cd4c5764405362395b7590BC8BC (accessed 14 August 2023).

mission to proclaim God's kingdom. Christendom appeared because converted rulers wanted to place their realm under the reign of Christ.[15] By the time of Constantine's death, the Roman Empire had become a 'universal Christian commonwealth embracing Armenians, Iberians, Arabs, and Aksumites' that would be preserved well into Byzantine history.[16] The success of the Church's proclamation, from Palestine to the Palatine Hill, from Britain to Byzantium, changed the Roman Empire for the better. But the resulting product, Christendom, was far from perfect. Christendom did not make the world the kingdom of heaven. Often it was the opposite: it manufactured a merciless hell for many on the margins. Bishops and princes got rich and fat off the suffering of others. This is the tension we must wrestle with in church history and in the story of Western civilisation.[17] Christendom, for all the cultivation of Christian virtues, for all the claim of the spirit's effervescent presence, for all the advances in human liberties from the Magna Carta to the Bill of Rights, was still tainted with the human capacity for evil. It is indubitably true that Christian civilisation was often neither Christian nor civil. At times, it seemed as if the kingdom of heaven was still very much in heaven and not on earth.

The result of this historical collusion between Church and empire forces us to come to terms with the sins of the imperial past. Should the US government pay reparations to the descendants of African American slaves whose ancestors were deprived of the income of their labours? What about a treaty between the Australian government and the native Aboriginal and Torres Strait islanders? Should the UK return the Rosetta Stone to Egypt, the Benin Bronzes to Nigeria, and the Koh-i-Noor diamond to India? The discussion of empire has become notoriously politicised, even in academia.

---

15 Oliver O'Donovan, *The Desire of the Nations: Rediscovering the roots of political theology* (Cambridge: Cambridge University Press, 1996), p. 195; James K. A. Smith, *Awaiting the King: Reforming public theology* (Grand Rapids, MI: Baker, 2017), p. 162.

16 Elizabeth Key Fowden, 'Constantine and the Peoples of the Eastern Frontier', in *The Cambridge Companion to the Age of Constantine*, ed. Noel Lenski (Cambridge: Cambridge University Press, 2006), p. 392.

17 See John Dickson, *Bullies and Saints: An honest look at the good and evil of Christian history* (Grand Rapids, MI: Zondervan, 2021).

Some speak of empire as if it is an obdurate demonic spirit that still lurks in the market squares and finds incarnation in the many statues and streets named after imperial colonisers such as Clive of India or President James Polk. In the minds of some activists, great nations such as the UK, France, Spain and the USA must be ritually exorcised of *imperium* so as to cleanse the consciences of the living of the sins of the imperial past. Others wish to view the former empires of Britain and Europe as morally complex but not entirely malevolent. Were there any perks to empire, even for the colonised? Shall we remember too the evils of the Arab, Mongol, Ottoman, Incan, Ashanti and Japanese empires? There is quite a vigorous debate going on about how we recognise the past, reconcile in the present and build for the future in the light of this often-dark imperial history.[18]

All of this goes back to Constantine. It was Constantine who ceased the persecution of Christians, who granted the churches privileges and gifts, and who even presided over the ecumenical council of Nicaea in AD 325. The authenticity of Constantine's faith has been a matter of concerted debate. Some suppose that Constantine's affection for Christianity was less a matter of revelation than it was of *Realpolitik*: he saw Christianity as a useful tool for controlling the empire. The reality is probably more complex. Constantine most likely had some devotion to one God in general and to Christ in particular. But Constantine perhaps admired the Christian God because he saw in this God a mirror of himself: one unrivalled and supreme lord of the world.

Accordingly, we must be careful about overly valorising Western civilisation and too eagerly lionising liberal democracy in the name of Christian triumphalism.

---

18 See e.g., Alexander J. Motyl, 'Is Everything Empire? Is Empire Everything?' *Comparative Politics* 39 (2006): 229–49; Kwasi Kwarteng, *Ghosts of Empire: Britain's legacies in the modern world* (New York: Public Affairs, 2011); William Dalrymple, *The Anarchy: The East India Company, corporate violence, and the pillage of an empire* (New York: Bloomsbury, 2019); Sathnam Sanghera, *Empireland: How imperialism has shaped modern Britain* (London: Viking, 2021); Nigel Biggar, *Colonialism: A moral reckoning* (London: William Colllins, 2023).

The riches of the West were acquired through the exploitation of African and Asian colonies. The insatiable thirst for wealth meant trading in slaves and opium. English Puritans such as George Whitefield could wax eloquently about the magnificent grace of God one morning, then in the evening urge audiences that it was their divine duty to subjugate and civilise the African 'negro'. Jonathan Edwards was a preacher of God's scandalous grace in America's Great Awakening, a tireless advocate for the education of indigenous Americans, yet he once wrote a sermon on the back of a receipt for the purchase of a slave. It's hard to explain to young people these days what the British East India Company did in India. It was the equivalent of Amazon.com raising an army, invading New Zealand, taxing the population into poverty, enslaving people into textile production, and then turning the country into a narco state to manufacture heroin for South America. The West was responsible for the Crusades, wars of religion, peasant uprisings, debtors' prisons, persecutions of the Jews, violent revolutions in France and Russia, two world wars, land clearances and stock market crashes. Christianity has often given sanction to greed, conquest, slavery, exploitation and the 'othering' of oppressed peoples.

Even our liberal democracies, built on notions of freedom, equality and the rule of law, are hardly the paragons of virtue we like to think they are. Many liberal democracies can still multiply injustices with racism, poverty, inequality and ecological recklessness. The ability of corporations – big tech, big pharma, the energy lobby, the gambling cartels – to buy politicians and influence legislation poses the question as to whether Western nations are ruled by the people or a plutocracy of CEOs. Some would argue that liberal democracy depends on continuous wars to create public enemies to unify a diversified population and to justify massive defence budgets that prop up the military–industrial complex.[19] Recent attempts to liberate places such as Iraq and Afghanistan from dictatorial rule in the name of spreading democracy succeeded only in unleashing

---

19 Stanley Hauerwas and William H. Willimon, *Resident Aliens: Life in the Christian colony* (Nashville, TN: Abingdon, 1989), pp. 35–6.

the sectarian chaos over which strong-armed leaders had kept a tight lid. Further, in many Western nations, 'Christianity' has been the religious underpinning to white nationalism. Or else, the churches within liberal democracies have been affluent to the point of being indifferent to the suffering of others. Even worse, what testimony does the Church have now when it has been revealed to have harboured sexual predators in its ranks and refused to expose them – something true of at least Catholics, Anglicans and Southern Baptists?

Even with acknowledging the sins of the past, there is a case to be made for the achievements of Christendom and for Western civilisation.[20] Whatever its failings, which are obviously many, Christendom gave us schools, academies, universities, hospitals, the Enlightenment, the rise of science, and notions of universal human rights, things that are impossible without Christianity being hardwired into the moral and intellectual DNA of the West. Christianity is the reason why the gladiatorial games ended and slave-markets were shut down. The pope's Christendom was preferable to Caesar's paganism. Western civilisation is still preferable to Communism and a caliphate.[21]

Yet within the West there is a tension. The Christians of the West were supposed by many to be building Jerusalem on earth. While some shards of heavenly light did shine through, on other occasions the construction seemed instead to resemble a cathedral of human depravity. Christendom often looked like a city of perdition rather than the city of God. Sad to say, with a few exceptions, it was empire rather than evangelism that made Christianity a global religion. Do we regard the Church's association with empire as a marriage of providential convenience or an act of spiritual adultery? Did Christ defeat Caesar or did we merely turn Christ into Caesar?

---

20 For contrasting evaluations of the Constantinian revolution that led to Christendom, see Stanley Hauerwas, *After Christendom? How the Church is to behave if freedom, justice, and a Christian nation are bad ideas* (Nashville, TN: Abingdon, 2011); and Peter Leithart, *Defending Constantine: The twilight of an empire and the dawn of Christendom* (Downers Grove, IL: InterVarsity Press, 2010).

21 On which, see Konstantin Kisin, *An Immigrant's Love Letter to the West* (London: Constable, 2022).

Of the mixing of religion and politics there is no end

Many will claim that the Church should never get involved in politics. The Church (such people will say) should not seek a place at the table of political power or even get involved in debates about civil rights, climate change and public housing. It's not the Church's business to go around singing the praises of the West, or yelling tirades against the West. Our Lord said, 'My kingdom is not of this world'[22] because the kingdom is spiritual and timeless, and belongs to the heavenly realm.[23] Many will wag a finger at us as meddlesome clergy planting their pulpit in places it does not belong. Keep your sermons in church, not Congress; worship your Lord far away from the House of Lords. Stick to the cure of souls, not trying to save the world!

Many have indeed argued that Christ's kingdom is a purely spiritual entity. But to our mind this is a gross distortion of what Jesus himself said to Pilate in John's Gospel:

> 'My kingdom isn't the sort that grows in this world,' replied Jesus. 'If my kingdom were from this world, my supporters would have fought, to stop me being handed over to the Judaeans. So then, my kingdom is not the sort that comes from here.'
> (John 18:36)

This translation captures something that many commentators gloss over. Yes, Jesus' kingdom is not like the kingdoms of this world. It doesn't originate the same way or behave like the kingdoms of this world. But Jesus' kingdom is still for this world, for the benefit and blessing of this world, for the redemption and rescue of this world. If Jesus were an earthly king of this age, then there would be soldiers killing to bring about his kingdom, just as they do for every

---

22 John 18:36 (NIV).
23 See Eusebius, *Church History* 3.19–20. Similarly, Justin, *First Apology* 11.

other earthly kingdom: victory through violence. Yet that's not how Jesus' kingdom will come. The kingdom will come rather through the imperial violence done to him on the cross and through the anti-imperial, death-reversing, justice-loving power of resurrection. Then the kingdom spreads, not through conquest, but through the spirit's life-giving and liberating power being experienced by more and more people and through their life-giving contributions to the world. At the heart of John's kingdom-theology is God's love revealed in the death of his Son, the Lamb, the Messiah. This is conquest, but by love. This is power, but in weakness. This is kingship, but in self-giving suffering for others. This kingdom is not one that arises from within the world. But as it advances, as it spreads, it dispels and displaces the dark forces in the world.[24]

If Jesus' kingdom is of such an order, not from this world but for this world, then keeping out of politics is impossible. We must be political in some sense because the kingdom of God has political implications for proclamation and poverty, for justice and judgement, for Congress and Church, for love and liberty. While Church and State are separable, there is always going to be a connection between religion and politics because of the intersection of values and voting. Religion is going to be part of the political conversation whether everyone likes it or not.

As Anglicans, we routinely get cornered by our Baptist friends who tell us that the Anglican arrangement, with the King as the supreme governor of the Church of England, and the Crown appointing bishops and key positions in the English Church, is a political abomination. Or worse, it is a rehash of the Constantinian corruption of power, grasping after a new Christendom while ignorant of the evils of the old one. The wall of separation between Church and State is good for Church and State, lest the two corrupt each other in some unholy theocratic alliance. So we are told ad nauseam.

---

24 See N. T. Wright, *How God Became King: Getting to the heart of the Gospels* (London: SPCK, 2012), pp. 144, 228–32; N. T. Wright, *History and Eschatology: Jesus and the promise of natural theology* (Waco, TX: Baylor University Press, 2019), p. 315 n. 2.

We are no fans of theocracy, nor of the divine right of kings. Yet when we hear that complaint, we always have a standard answer. Yes, you want to avoid the evils of Constantine and Christendom. Instead of seeking influence in the halls of power, you want to be the angry prophet on the margins speaking truth to power. All well and good. But what happens when the power listens? What happens when the power or the people ask you to sit on a committee, contribute to an investigation, run a programme, advise on policy, or serve as a chaplain? That kind of absolute separation of Church and State is fine if you want to be a critic making snarky criticisms on the sidelines. But if you want to change the game you need skin in the game. The people who change history must make history. If you want to build for the kingdom, then you have to build something: relationships, alliances, advocacy, food banks, para-church ministries, youth clubs, foreign aid programmes. You need to be in the room where it happens.

Building for Christ and his kingdom today

In this book, we are trying to answer some questions. How do you build for the kingdom in an age of empire, where totalitarians tyrannise and our democracies appear dysfunctional? This is not a purely religious question; it is also a contemporary political matter. Back in 2019, Guy Verhofstadt of the European Union declared that the answer to the UK's problems was to join a mighty European empire. The Dutch politician said:

> The world order of tomorrow is not a world order based on nation states or countries. It's a world order that is based on empires.
>
> China is not a nation; it's a civilisation.
>
> India, you know it better than I do, is not a nation. There are 2,000 nations in India. There are 20 different languages that are used there. There are four big religions at the same time, and its 2011 census recorded five regions with more than five million inhabitants. It is the biggest democracy worldwide.

The U.S. is also an empire, more than a nation. Maybe tomorrow they will speak more Spanish than English; I don't know what will happen.

And then finally, the Russian Federation.

The world of tomorrow is a world of empires, in which we Europeans and you British can only defend your interests, your way of life, by doing it together in a European framework and a European Union.[25]

While we love Europe, we are highly resistant to the idea that a European empire is the solution to Europe's problems (even more so if you know that the German word for 'empire' is *Reich*!). We believe instead in building for the kingdom of Jesus, not a social gospel, not a theocratic monarch with a magical sword, neither agrarian anarchism nor neo-liberal economics. What we believe in is a theo-political gospel that declares that Jesus is Lord and Caesar is not, and Jesus' kingdom is about forgiveness and freedom to flourish as renewed human beings. What does that kind of kingdom look like among Ukrainian refugees huddled together in a Polish church? What does that kingdom mean for a pastor who saw a video featuring members of his congregation waving confederate flags inside the Capitol building on 6 January 2021? What does it mean to pray 'may it be on earth as it is in heaven' in an age of authoritarian regimes and democratic chaos?

We are not offering a full-blown political theology, solving every controversial topic from abortion to climate change to religious liberty. But we believe Christians should be committed to the politics of divine love, that is, love for God and love for neighbour. We are of the conviction that the kingdom means seeing people come to Jesus in faith, just as much as it means advocating for a world where everyone can 'sit under their own vines and under their own fig trees, and no one shall make them afraid'.[26] Or, to

25 Ben Johnson, 'Only an EU "Empire" Can Secure Liberty: EU Leader', *Acton Institute*, 16 September 2019: https://www.acton.org/publications/transatlantic/2019/09/16/only-eu-empire-can-secure-liberty-eu-leader (accessed 15 August 2023).

26 Micah 4:4; cf. Zechariah 3:10.

use the words of a favourite Christmas hymn, 'In His name all oppression shall cease.'[27] For the Christian hope is that all oppression,
whether by political actors, or by powers of the present darkness,
will be pacified and reconciled to the one who is King of kings.

---

27 Placide Cappeau, 'O Holy Night' (1847), trans. John Sullivan Dwight.

3

Power and the 'Powers' in Early Christianity: John, Paul and the Paradox of Biblical Politics

A Coronation Bible reading

On Saturday 6 May 2023, a television audience of many millions watched as Rishi Sunak, the British prime minister (and a practising Hindu), set the tone for the Coronation of King Charles III by reading a passage from Paul's letter to the Colossians. The passage reminded the new king, and the watching world, of the ultimate kingdom:

> Giving thanks unto the Father, which hath made us meet to be partakers of the inheritance of the saints in light: who hath delivered us from the power of darkness, and hath translated us into the kingdom of his dear Son: in whom we have redemption through his blood, even the forgiveness of sins: who is the image of the invisible God, the firstborn of every creature: for by him were all things created, that are in heaven, and that are in earth, visible and invisible, whether they be thrones, or dominions, or principalities, or powers: all things were created by him, and for him: and he is before all things, and by him all things consist.[1]

---

1 Colossians 1:12–17 in the King James Version, used on that occasion.

This message is reinforced visually in the text from the book of Revelation inscribed above the high altar in Westminster Abbey. The new king would have had a close-up view of these words as he was crowned and anointed: 'The kingdoms of this world are become the kingdoms of our Lord, and of his Christ.'[2]

At least some of the millions watching that day must have scratched their heads in puzzlement at the apparent accumulation of irony. Is Jesus really the King, or is the new British monarch the king? How can it make sense to say that 'both' are king – as the event seemed to be claiming? And, out beyond that, does not the whole thing appear to be an intolerable mixture of 'religion' and 'politics', something which many in recent centuries have declared to be dangerous, unworkable and bad for society as a whole?

To address this, and thereby to provide some further biblical foundations for the subject of the rule of Jesus and the place of the 'powers' of the world, we want to look in more detail at two New Testament books, in both of which we see, from a modern Western perspective, an apparent irony not unlike that which many perceived in the Coronation liturgy. We shall return to Colossians presently, to ponder how on earth Paul, languishing in prison, can say that Jesus is the one in and through whom all principalities and powers came to exist. But we begin with an equally puzzling passage in John's Gospel.

All 'authority' is from God

As the Fourth Gospel reaches its sustained climax, with Jesus facing Pontius Pilate (the kingdom of God confronting the kingdoms of the world!), one sentence stands out as articulating the biblical paradox of power and politics. Pontius Pilate, irritated by Jesus' failure to respond to his questions, challenges him:

---

2   Revelation 11:15, also King James Version. The Greek, literally translated, simply reads, 'The kingdom [singular] of the world has become of our Lord and of his Christ.'

'Aren't you going to speak to me?' he said. 'Don't you know that I have the authority to let you go, and the authority to crucify you?'

'You couldn't have any authority at all over me,' replied Jesus, 'unless it was given to you from above. That's why the person who handed me over to you is guilty of a greater sin.'[3]

Let that sink in for a moment: *Jesus, the Word incarnate, the Son of Man, the Messiah, acknowledges that the pagan governor Pontius Pilate has a God-given authority over him.* The Jesus who had declared that the world's judgement was now on the way;[4] the Jesus who assured his followers that he had himself defeated the world[5] – this Jesus recognises that a second-rate Roman magistrate is in a position of divinely authorised responsibility and authority *over him*.

Of course, Jesus adds a vital rider. Those to whom authority and responsibility are given will be held accountable, and that accountability works outwards to include any who put the authority-figures in the position of doing the wrong thing. Jesus – and John, of course – assume that what Pilate is about to do, sending Jesus to his death, is indeed the wrong thing: it is a 'sin'. It will be blamed on those mainly responsible, in other words (we assume) the chief priests who have presented Pilate with a strange prisoner and an even stranger set of charges against him.

Before going any further, two preliminary conclusions suggest themselves. First, Jesus is portrayed as endorsing the wider biblical view (about which more anon) that God the Creator desires and intends his world to be run by human authorities. Of course, a full statement of this biblical principle would add that God intends the authorities to act with wisdom and justice, paying special attention to the needs of the poor and vulnerable. But the point remains: rulers, even when foolish and unjust, appear to hold a God-given authority.

---

3   John 19:11.
4   John 12:31–2.
5   John 16:33.

This is balanced, second, by the rider: those in authority will be held to account. This would not have come as a surprise to John's non-Jewish readers, some of whom at least would be used to the idea of magistrates being put on trial after their term of office. Nor would it surprise Jewish readers, whose Scriptures contained many oracles of divine judgement on wicked rulers. Saying that the authorities are appointed and authorised by God does not mean that God endorses whatever they then do. (That fallacy occurs in modern democracies, when winning an election is said to give the victors a mandate and reason to act with carte blanche.) The biblical view is that God holds his appointed authorities to account for their actions. A classic example is in Isaiah 10, where God first appoints the Assyrians to punish his people and then punishes the Assyrians themselves for the arrogant spirit with which they carried out the task.

The first point is rooted in the story of creation itself, set out in Genesis 1 and 2 and refocused by Psalm 8. Without going into detail, it seems obvious – from the creation of humans in God's image, given human authority over the animals – that the Creator intends his world to be run *through obedient human beings*. That was part of the deep structure of creation's design. The idea of humans reflecting the divine image is actually the democratisation, on the part of Israel's Scriptures, of the well-known ancient view that kings and other rulers were made 'in the image of the god'. It made sense, after all: the god was in overall charge, but the human ruler, with delegated authority, made and enforced the laws. Many at the time will have seen this, as many have done more recently, as a convenient and self-serving fiction on the part of a scribal elite, producing official texts for a royal master. The Hebrew Scriptures offer a different kind of critique: *all humans*, not only rulers, *bear the divine image.*[6]

That is reaffirmed, without the 'image' language but with clear echoes of Genesis 1, in Psalm 8. The psalm begins and ends with

---

6 On the significance of ancient Near Eastern context for reading Genesis 1:27–8 about the 'image of God', see Michael F. Bird, *Evangelical Theology: A biblical and systematic introduction*, 2nd edn (Grand Rapids, MI: Zondervan, 2020), pp. 749–51.

a strong, delighted affirmation of YHWH's supreme authority: 'O YHWH, our Sovereign, how majestic is your name in all the earth!'[7]

But contemplation of God's creation then leads to the question of what humans are and why God appears to take a special interest in them. What are humans? What is 'a son of man' (literal translation)?[8] The answer is that they appear to hold a strange, delegated authority, under the overall rule of the sovereign YHWH. They seem to be poised between heaven and earth, designed to reflect God's authority into his world:

> You have made them a little lower than God
> and crowned them with glory and honour.
> You have given them dominion over the works of
> your hands;
> you have put all things under their feet . . .'[9]

When, in the fullness of time, Paul writes of those who receive God's covenant mercies as 'reigning in life', or when Revelation declares that those redeemed by the Lamb's blood become 'a kingdom and priests to our God' who 'will reign on the earth', they are picking up not only the vocation of Israel ('kingdom of priests') but the vocation of Adam and Eve ('dominion . . . over every living thing').[10] This is what humans were made for. All Christian reflection on human power and authority – in other words, all attempts to articulate a Christian mind on questions of politics – must operate within this framework.

By the time of Paul and Revelation, of course, the human vocation had been reaffirmed through the specifically human achievement of Jesus himself. Thus Paul, in the Colossians passage, describes Jesus first and foremost as 'the image of the invisible God': the truly human one, in other words. John, meanwhile, well aware of what he's

---

7   Psalm 8:1, 9.

8   Psalm 8:4. Most modern translations avoid the gender-specific phrase 'son of man' here, preferring something like 'human beings'; but granted Jesus' use of it, it may be better to allow the echoes to be heard.

9   Psalm 8:5–6.

10 See Romans 5:17; Revelation 5:10 (cf. 1:6; 20:6); Exodus 19:6 (and 23:22 LXX); Genesis 1:28.

doing, has Pontius Pilate declaring 'Here's the man.'[11] John is thereby looking back to his own prologue, where the phrase 'the Word
became flesh'[12] is the equivalent, in John's 'new Genesis', of the creation of humans in God's image.[13]

In neither case is the emphasis on Jesus' human role intended in any way to diminish or modify belief in his personal embodiment of Israel's God. Paul is clear that in Jesus all the divine fullness
was glad to dwell. John, likewise, introduces Jesus as the Word who
was indeed God.[14] But this in no way undermines or relativises Jesus' full humanity or reduces its vital ongoing significance. To suppose that it did would be to miss the point – the point that was clear in
the Hebrew Bible but opaque to those who, from comparatively early
in the Church, tried to fit the scriptural hurricane into the bottle of
Greek philosophy.

It is ultimately this biblical vision of Jesus, paradoxical as it still appears to many, that lies at the heart of the puzzle of power and politics.
We ought not to be surprised that the question of how the Creator's authority and activity relates to the authority and activity of human rulers raises the same kind of issue as the question of the mutual relation
between the 'divinity' and 'humanity' of Jesus. Of course, the two questions are not simply parallel, though in many ways they are that too.
If Jesus is the model for how divine authority works in the world, he
is also the conduit through which that authority flows. That is part of
what Paul is saying in Colossians. To this we shall return.

The human role – and the human problem

The story of all this, as set out in Israel's Scriptures, became more
complex because the image-bearers decided to do things differ-

---

11 John 19:5.

12 John 1:14.

13 Explored further in N. T. Wright, 'History, Eschatology and New Creation in the Fourth
    Gospel', in *Interpreting Jesus: Essays on the Gospels* (London: SPCK; Grand Rapids, MI:
    Zondervan, 2020), ch. 16.

14 Colossians 1:19; 2:9; John 1:1–3.

ently. Genesis 3 could serve as an allegory for (among many other things!) the notorious corruption of power. Given authority over God's world, the humans tried to use it for their own advantage. The results were clear: exile from the garden, the Flood, the half-built tower and the confusion of tongues (Genesis 3 – 11). But – and again this points ahead to the paradox of politics – the Creator did not unmake the original purpose. The somewhat sterile later debate about whether 'the divine image' was 'lost' in the Fall needs to be recalibrated not just in terms of what humans *are* but in terms of what they are called to *do*: not so much ontology as vocation.[15] In those terms, the call to reflect God into his world has clearly not been rescinded. Faced with disaster, God calls a human, Noah, to engineer the immediate rescue operation. He then calls Abraham to be his partner in the slow, painful work of new creation itself. The human vocation is not abrogated: God still desires and intends to work in his world *through obedient humans,* and he continues to do so even when that obedience is at best patchy.

In Abraham's case the problem quickly becomes clear. Abraham is faithful one minute, faithless the next. His children, grand-children and great-grandchildren are no better. But the reason the story exists at all is because of the ancient, tenacious Israelite belief that God the Creator, having set up his world so that it would work through human beings, did not abandon that project – just as he did not abandon the Israel-project, the call of Abraham's family to bring blessing to the world, just because of Israel's long-predicted failure. In long hindsight, the New Testament authors might point out that God could not abandon the project. It was, and had always been, a plan designed for his own personal use – as would eventually become clear.

From the start, then, the Creator's intention was for humans to bring God's wise order into the world. Even after the Fall, there was to be no question of unchecked anarchy, 'holy' or otherwise. God's grief over widespread wickedness occasioned the Flood.[16] We recall,

---

15 This has been well argued by, among others, J. R. Middleton, *The Liberating Image: The 'Imago Dei' in Genesis 1* (Grand Rapids, MI: Brazos Press, 2005).

16 Genesis 6:5–7.

too, the scorn and distaste of the author of Judges: 'There was no king in Israel,' he writes, and so 'all the people did what was right in their own eyes'.[17] That, it was implied, was the political equivalent of the nation going back to *tohu wa-bohu*, the formless and void state which corresponded to the pre-creation waters in Genesis 1:2 and indeed to devastated Jerusalem in Jeremiah's vision.[18] The book of Judges wasted no time on subtle hints: what was needed, the writer was saying, was a human being, an image-bearer, a royal figure, to come and reflect the Creator's wise, healing justice into the world, into Israel.

But of course – almost as though the later writers wanted to accuse the author of Judges of hopeless naivety! – from the start Israel's monarchy was every bit as ambiguous as Abraham himself: faithful one minute, faithless the next. Samuel had warned against the idea of kingship, seeing it as a rejection of God's own sovereignty. Then, when the people insisted, he painted a bleak (but sadly accurate) portrait of how monarchy would work out.[19] The ambiguity continued with God's choice of David to replace the feckless Saul. David was the man after God's own heart, the recipient of extraordinary dynastic promises through which God's purpose (to come and dwell for ever in the midst of his people) would be fulfilled;[20] but David failed even more spectacularly than Saul. Solomon succeeded him, but his wise learning was not matched by his worshipping loyalty. His collusion with idolatry resulted in the kingdom being divided. Good (though not unflawed) kings followed from time to time – Asa, Hezekiah, Josiah – but the books of Samuel and Kings tell a story of the long entailments of Genesis 3. The people who were supposed to be reflecting God's wise and just rule into the life of the people and the world routinely got it wrong. The result, as with Adam and Eve, was exile, just as Moses himself had warned.[21]

---

17 Judges 21:25; also 17:6. On there being 'no king', see too 18:1; 19:1.
18 Jeremiah 4:23.
19 1 Samuel 8:4–18.
20 1 Samuel 13:14; 2 Samuel 7.12–16.
21 Deuteronomy 28:58–68.

The problem of political power – even among the people of God, let alone in the wider non-Israelite world – is thus a major theme of the Old Testament. This is the necessary background for understanding what Paul, John and the other early Christians say, with characteristic density, about the 'powers' – and for thinking wisely about what it all might mean for today.

One could offer a rough and ready summary of where we have got to so far. To put it negatively: anarchy is hopeless, because the bullies will always prey on the weak (so God therefore intends his world to be governed by humans). But authority is problematic, because the vocation to rule constitutes a temptation to abuse power (so God will hold authorities to account). All this is on display, again and again, throughout the Bible, but as an open-ended story, indicating that the Creator's last word has not yet been spoken. And that last word will itself emerge from within the parameters already set in Genesis 1 and 2 and Psalm 8 (the human vocation), Genesis 12 – 22 (the Abrahamic vocation) and not least Psalms 2, 72, 132, 2 Samuel 7 and the messianic passages in Isaiah (the Davidic vocation). If the world is to be held to account, it will be through a human; through an Israelite; through a Davidic king. One could say that this is one of the questions, deep rooted in Israel's Scriptures, to which the New Testament offers a clear answer.

Of course, the royal psalms that celebrate the wise rule of the Davidic king can themselves be seen, like the plaintive refrain in Judges, as simply serving the interests of this or that Israelite monarch. No doubt they were sometimes used that way. But as they stand, they hold out the promise of a coming king who would at last overthrow idolatry, bring peace to the warring nations, and in particular come to the rescue of widows and orphans, the oppressed and the stranger. Psalm 72 is perhaps the clearest statement of this theme of saving, healing justice: a prayer for YHWH, the Creator, to give his justice, his character of putting-things-right, to the king, so that the king will 'defend the cause of the poor of the people, give deliverance to the needy, and crush the oppressor'. This royal justice will bring about a worldwide rule of peace and prosperity. Just as King Solomon had built the Temple so that the divine glory would come and fill it, so this reign of wise, healing justice would cause the divine glory to fill the whole earth.[22]

But how? Some of the royal psalms celebrated a coming victory in nakedly violent terms:

You shall break them with a rod of iron
and dash them in pieces like a potter's vessel.

The Lord is at your right hand;
he will shatter kings on the day of his wrath.
He will execute judgement among the nations,
filling them with corpses;
he will shatter heads
over the wide earth.[23]

This could easily be the emphasis picked up by later readers, not least those who knew the book of Daniel. There, the 'little' horn that utters proud blasphemies against the Most High will have its dominion taken away, 'consumed and totally destroyed', leaving the way clear for the worldwide kingship and dominion to be 'given to the people of the holy ones of the Most High'.[24] Many first-century readers of Daniel took this to refer to a coming military victory against the pagans – as well they might, granted the popular memory, kept fresh by the festival of Hanukkah, of the Maccabean triumph against the Syrians. The book of Daniel, indeed, provides plenty of material for anyone interested in how the powers of the world were seen in the pre-Christian Jewish world. Again and again, the pagan rulers do their worst and Israel's God, 'the God of heaven', rescues his faithful people. The climactic scenes in chapters 2 and 7, interpreted messianically in the first century (as Josephus bears oblique witness), make it clear what is going on. God will vindicate his faithful people despite their suffering. And he will

22 Psalm 72:4, 19; compare Isaiah 11:1–10.
23 Psalm 2:9; 110:5–6. These psalms (though not these verses) are frequently cited in the NT.
24 Daniel 7:8, 25–7.

do so not only through that suffering but also through military or quasi-military victory.

But there is another strand of ancient biblical thought which offers a radically different vision of how the coming Davidic king will overcome the powers of the world and establish a reign of justice and peace. The long sequence of poems embedded in the canonical book of Isaiah focuses the promise of royal deliverance[25] on the work of YHWH's Servant,[26] and then on the picture of the victorious heavenly warrior.[27] This is not the place to discuss the original meaning of these remarkable passages or the various traditions, ancient and modern, of their interpretation. It is sufficient to say that, in early Christian reflection, following arguably from the teaching of Jesus himself, the passages about the 'suffering Servant' in particular were taken as the vital clue to understanding how the messianic victory over the forces of evil was accomplished. It was through this strange figure, the king who was also the servant, who was also (it seems) the 'arm' of YHWH himself. The servant was to embody *both* the vocation of Israel *and* the vocation – so to say – of Israel's God, and thereby take upon himself the weight of exile, shame and death, in order to renew the covenant with Israel and thereby renew creation itself. Victory over the dark powers, particularly those conjured up by the idolatry which the prophets condemned not only in the pagan nations but also in Israel itself, would come through Israel's God, the Creator, fulfilling in person the multi-layered vocation of the king, and of Israel itself, and ultimately of true humanity. All that, we may surmise, stands in the background of what John and Paul are saying when they sketch, with tantalising brevity, their picture of Jesus and the 'powers'.

So what are the 'powers'?

But what are these 'powers'? Paul lists several in Colossians 1: 'thrones and lordships and rulers and powers'. A similar list in

---

25 Isaiah 9:2–7; 11:1–10.

26 Isaiah 42:1–9; 49:1–13; 50:4–9; 52:13 – 53:12.

27 Isaiah 61:1–11; 63:1–6.

Ephesians declares that Jesus is lord over all 'rule and authority and power and lordship', and over 'every name that is invoked, both in the present age and also in the age to come'.[28] That obviously includes both what we would call 'earthly' or 'political' rulers and what we might call any 'non-human' or 'supernatural' quasi-personal 'forces' that stand behind the 'earthly' rulers. They already feature prominently in significant biblical contexts such as Deuteronomy 32, Isaiah 14 and arguably Daniel 7.[29] Then, in a famous passage in Romans 8, we find 'death . . . life . . . angels . . . rulers . . . the present . . . the future . . . powers . . . height . . . depth' – with Paul adding 'any other creature', not only in case he'd left anything out but in order to remind us that all these things are precisely *creatures*, part of God's world, not independent divine or quasi-divine beings.[30] It is possible to tease out particular meanings for all these terms, but the fact that Paul can mix the lists around is a fair indication that he is more concerned to stress the lordship of Jesus over all 'powers' of whatever sort than to provide specific definitions or discrete categories.[31]

The point about the 'powers' is that, in Paul's world, they are both (what we would call) 'earthly' and (what we would call) 'heavenly' or 'supernatural'. Those terms are slippery. We perceive them through the lens of modern Western thought, in which a great gulf stands between the present world of space, time and matter and any other, whether we call it 'heavenly' or 'spiritual' or anything else – or indeed whether, like the sceptics and rationalists, we sweep such categories off the table as so much metaphysical nonsense. Many have debated whether Paul is referring simply to earthly 'powers' such as emperors and magistrates, or to non-earthly powers such as angels or demons – as though he lived in a world where one could easily distinguish the one from the other, and where anyone referring to them ought to be able to state which was which

---

28 Ephesians 1:21.

29 See e.g., Deuteronomy 32:16–17; Isaiah 14:12–23; Daniel 7:1–28.

30 Romans 8:38–9.

31 For the details, see Walter Wink, *The Powers*, 3 vols (Philadelphia, PA and Minneapolis, MN: Fortress, 1984, 1986, 1992).

and how they were related. No such gulf between ontological levels existed for ancient thinkers, except for the small minority who embraced Epicureanism. (Indeed, it is the runaway success of modern forms of Epicureanism that pushes us automatically – until we stop and think about it – towards a rigid separation between the two spheres).[32] For Paul, the visible world and the invisible overlapped in all sorts of ways. Anything in creation that is worshipped instead of the Creator God has the capacity to become an idol. And when Paul discusses idols and their temples, he explains that there you will find demons – malevolent discarnate beings bent on corrupting and distorting human life and work – eager to recruit more humans to their deadly pursuits. The 'gods' themselves are nonexistent, in the sense that there is no ultimate reality corresponding to the words 'Zeus', 'Ares' or 'Aphrodite'. But when people go into the temples dedicated to these fictitious entities, they lay themselves open to the shadowy sub-personal and dehumanising influence of the demons. Paul is quite restrained in what he says at this point. Some writers of the Second Temple period were less so. But if he holds back from detailed speculation, he is clear enough about the reality of quasi-personal forces of evil.

The cult of Rome and Caesar, increasingly popular in the mid first century precisely in the areas where Paul spent most time, was a classic example of a 'power' which crossed the categories. Caesar was a real and powerful man; Rome was a real and powerful city; but the 'power' they wielded was more than the sum total of their ability to give orders and have them obeyed, or to establish the official norms by which most people in the Mediterranean world would structure their lives. We with our post-Enlightenment split universe don't have good language for this kind of 'power'. We talk about economic 'pressures' or political 'forces', which seem to mean more than simply 'the markets won't let us do that' or 'policies like that won't win many votes'. We might talk about 'the spirit of the age' or about 'collective delusions' or worse. Some who lived

---

32 On this, see N. T. Wright, *History and Eschatology: Jesus and the promise of natural theology* (Waco, TX: Baylor University Press, 2019), esp. ch. 1.

through the horrors of mid-twentieth-century Europe spoke of the dark mood that gripped Germany in the 1930s, making it easy for a great many people to believe certain things, however untrue and wicked they were, and almost impossible for them to think or believe certain other things, however wise and healthy they were. Perhaps such questions only become fully clear with hindsight. Perhaps the widespread lies of any particular generation are ignored because, like the mountain outside the back door, they are simply part of the regular horizon, and so fail to register.

As to the 'existence' of non-human 'forces' and their destructive capability: those who have worked in what is now cautiously referred to as 'deliverance ministry' return from that dark vocation with tales of convoluted webs of deceit – particularly self-deceit – and of the ways in which shadowy 'forces' seem to lure people into situations and behaviours where they appear to be under some kind of extraneous influence, and do real harm to themselves and others. And those who have lived and worked in places and cultures where worship of many gods is the norm speak credibly of destructive powers that can envelop and terrorise communities, families and individuals.

Such reflections form a surrounding context for what Paul says about rulers, thrones, authorities, dominions and so on, and also for what John has Jesus say (in a passage we shall shortly examine) about 'the ruler of this world'. From Caesar on his throne to the local officials and magistrates running a particular town or city, the early churches lived within complex webs of power. Jesus himself lived within those same complex webs, and, as we saw, acknowledged not only that Pontius Pilate had authority to order his execution but that this authority had been entrusted to him by God himself. But both Paul and John insisted that Jesus had achieved something previously unthinkable. He had won the decisive victory over the 'principalities' and 'powers', and was now enthroned as Lord of both heaven and earth. This places the question of the Church's relation to the 'powers' – of whatever sort – in a special spotlight. Something has changed. But what? And where does it now leave those who follow Jesus?

Jesus' victory over the powers

To answer these questions, we turn first to the passages that speak of the 'victory'. In John's Gospel, Jesus speaks of judgement being passed on 'this world's ruler'. The context is a typically Johannine convoluted discussion, beginning when some Greeks visiting Jerusalem for Passover ask to see Jesus. Instead of granting their request, Jesus regards it as the sign that 'the time has come . . . for the son of man to be glorified' (12:23). This means, apparently, (1) that the time has come for him to suffer, a suffering from which he naturally shrinks (12:27); (2) it is through that suffering and death that the 'glorification' will take place; (3) in that 'glorification', that is, through his death, Jesus will break the grip of 'this world's ruler' on those presently in its power, in other words, on the Gentile world, which will then be set free to worship the true God; and thus (4) the Greeks, like everybody else, will thereby be drawn to Jesus: 'Now comes the judgement of this world! Now this world's ruler is going to be thrown out! And when I've been lifted up from the earth, I will draw all people to myself.'[33]

That sets the terms within which we are then to read the entire sequence of events from John 13 through to Jesus' death in chapter 19, including his comment about Pontius Pilate's God-given authority. Jesus warns his followers of his imminent arrest, using the same phrase for the soldiers that he used for the one who would be 'cast out' because of his death: 'the ruler of the world is coming,' he said (14:30). It makes no sense, in my view, to separate this from the satanic takeover of Judas in the previous chapter (13:2, 30) or from the arrival of the soldiers in the garden (18:3), leading to the sequence of trials and then to the crucifixion. *And through all this Jesus claims that he is winning the victory over the powers of the world.* 'You'll have trouble in the world,' he says. 'But cheer up! I have defeated the world!' (16:33).

This can only mean that in Jesus' mind – and also clearly in John's, but the thought is so stupendous and new that it makes far

---

33 John 12:31–2.

more sense historically to suppose that John was simply reflecting the world-changing vision of Jesus himself – the crucifixion was the means of *victory over the powers of the world*. So much of the gospel story is about Jesus as Messiah. One of the central things the Messiah had to do was to win the victory over the dark powers that threatened God's people and God's world. This, according to John, is how he does it.[34] In characteristic style, John does not draw attention to this theme hereafter, but it is left to be inferred from the story he tells. Pilate, the present representative of the 'world's ruler', acts out his 'authority' by having Jesus killed. But the God who delegated that authority to Pilate reverses the verdict by raising Jesus from the dead and launching the world mission of his followers. John presents the whole sequence as the dramatic unveiling-in-action of *love*, which in Scripture was ascribed, not to the Messiah, but rather to Israel's God. The Word made flesh, the true human being, has brought together the two vocations, of the human who will put God's purposes into effect and of God himself, returning to dwell among his people in healing, rescuing love. The theme of 'new creation' that permeates the resurrection narratives of chapters 20 and 21 answers to the biblical promises in the Psalms and Isaiah of the new world to be born once the dark anti-creation forces have been defeated.

The same picture emerges dramatically from Colossians. The great poem in chapter 1 brings together two moments, 'creation' and 'reconciliation', without explaining either why 'reconciliation' was necessary or, in any detail, how it was accomplished (by 'the blood of his cross' is the only hint). Thus the opening statement of creation-through-the-image, the passage read by the Prime Minister at the Coronation, is set in poetic parallel to the statement of reconciliation:

He is the image of God, the invisible one,
The firstborn of all creation,

---

34 This whole theme, of 'atonement' accomplished by means of 'victory through substitution', is explored in N. T. Wright, *The Day the Revolution Began: Rethinking the meaning of Jesus' crucifixion* (London: SPCK; San Francisco: HarperOne, 2016).

For in him all things were created,
In the heavens and here on the earth.
Things we can see and things we cannot –
Thrones and lordships and rulers and powers –
All things were created both through him and for
    him ...
He is the start of it all,
Firstborn from realms of the dead;
So in all things he might be the chief.
For in him all the Fullness was glad to dwell
And through him to reconcile all to himself,
Making peace through the blood of his cross,
Through him – yes, things on the earth,
And also the things in the heavens.[35]

The poem draws together in complex and subtle ways the themes of creation and 'wisdom', of Genesis 1 and Proverbs 8, in order to tell the story of Jesus as Israel's Messiah and also as the living embodiment of Israel's God. It acclaims Jesus, described in the previous verses as '[God's] beloved son', as the one in, through and for whom all things were created, including all the 'powers' of the world: the same point that was made so sharply by Jesus himself to Pilate. God the Creator wanted his world to be wisely governed, as it were, *from within*, by his image-bearing human creatures. Indeed, that delegated authority is one of the primary meanings of 'image-bearing'. Jesus is the one, lately revealed, for whom the whole creational purpose had been waiting: creation, and now redemption, were projects designed for God's own use, and God incarnate has come to take up that rightful role.

But why does creation – complete with all its powers, both earthly and heavenly – need to be 'reconciled'? Clearly, the second half

---

35 Colossians 1:15–16, 18b–20. Vv. 17–18a form a separate poem-within-the-poem. On the whole passage, see N. T. Wright, *The Climax of the Covenant: Christ and the law in Pauline theology* (Edinburgh: T&T Clark, 1991; Minneapolis, MN: Fortress, 1992), ch. 5; *Paul and the Faithfulness of God* (London: SPCK; Minneapolis, MN: Fortress, 2013), pp. 672–7.

of the poem presupposes something not said here, something corresponding both to Genesis 3 – 11 and to the long story of humankind's failure, of Israel's failure. These multiple disasters have led to the point where the 'principalities' and 'powers', though created in, through and for the one we now know as Jesus, had accrued terrible power to themselves through human idolatry, and were now on the rampage through creation, wreaking havoc with people's lives and with God's world. They needed to be brought into line: to be 'reconciled'. But how?

Paul's answer, given in the next chapter in the context of warning the young church in Colossae against any repeat of what had happened in Galatia, is to describe Jesus' *defeat* of the 'principalities' and 'powers'.[36] The powers that stand behind the regulations even of Torah itself, and that now work through them to keep Gentiles out of the people of God despite the fact that the Messiah's death has dealt with their sins, have been done away with:

He [God] blotted out the handwriting that was against us, opposing us with its legal demands. He took it right out of the way, by nailing it to the cross. He stripped the rulers and authorities of their armor, and displayed them contemptuously to public view, celebrating his triumph over them in him.[37]

Here there comes into view, just as in John, one of the key elements of Paul's vision of the messianic victory. God's plan was (as he says in Ephesians 1:10) to sum up the whole cosmos in the Messiah, things in heaven and things on earth. And the coming together of Jew and Gentile in the gospel, breaking down the walls of ethnic and national identity in the process, through the forgiveness of the 'sins' that kept sinners enslaved to the 'powers', was a key gospel-driven sign of that eventual purpose (Ephesians 2:11–22). (This is parallel to Jesus' hint in John 12 that, though the Greeks could not approach at the moment, they would be drawn to him

---

36 On the context of Colossians and the polemical force of chapter 2, see Wright, *Paul and the Faithfulness of God*, pp. 992–5.

37 Colossians 2:14–15.

once in his death he had thrown out the 'world's ruler', the dark power that was keeping the nations apart.) Thus, insofar as Torah itself, the holy and God-given law of Israel, was separating believing Jews and believing Gentiles, it had been taken over by the dark forces that had been opposed to the Creator's purpose of new creation. As such, it had to be set aside.[38]

As often in Paul, this results in multiple ironies. The purpose of Israel – and of Torah as its charter – was to set forward the larger purposes of God the Creator. But insofar as Torah (or those who might be using it to this end) was now threatening to prevent those larger purposes from being fulfilled, it must be abolished – not in the sense of leaving God's people with no moral compass, but in the sense of inviting them, as people who were once idolaters but are so no more, into a larger multi-ethnic reality no longer defined by the restrictions (circumcision, food laws, Sabbaths) that in the ancient world marked out the Jews from their pagan neighbours. It takes all of Galatians to spell this out more fully, and even then it remains dense and challenging.[39]

But the ironies persist. Anyone witnessing Jesus' crucifixion would of course have said that the principalities and powers (the Roman soldiers and the shadowy demonic 'forces' that stood behind them) were celebrating a triumph over Jesus himself. But no: the resurrection compels Paul to see the picture the other way round. Jesus himself had stripped the rulers and authorities of their armour. He had held them up to public contempt. Exactly as in John: 'now this world's ruler is going to be thrown out.' Paul never provides his readers with a single all-inclusive statement of what Jesus' crucifixion accomplished. Every time he mentions it, he comes at it from a different angle. The cross remains a vast, dark mystery, not least because evil itself is a dark mystery, making no sense within God's good world. But at its heart, John and Paul both

---

38 There are strong parallels here with the argument of Romans 7, on which see Tom Wright, *Into the Heart of Romans: A deep dive into Paul's greatest letter* (London: SPCK; Grand Rapids, MI: Zondervan, 2023), ch. 2.

39 See N. T. Wright, *Galatians*, Commentaries for Christian Formation (Grand Rapids, MI: Eerdmans, 2021).

insist (much like John of Patmos in Revelation 5) that the cross was the victory, accomplished through Israel's Messiah taking the people's sins upon himself, that was required for the Creator's purposes to go ahead. Only so could humans at last be free to be the 'royal priesthood' through whom God's wise, healing justice would be brought into the world, resulting in new creation in the ultimate future and advance signs of that new creation even in the present. The principalities and powers had been hell-bent on maintaining their stranglehold on the world, not least by luring people into worshipping idols and thereby handing over to those idols – or whatever shadowy powers were using them as a 'front' – their proper image-bearing power. The result was to divide people of all sorts against one another: Jew from Greek, slave from free, male from female, with numerous subcategories stretching as far as the eye could see. The 'powers' were still in charge.

That is why Jesus' victory is celebrated in terms of the coming together, in the worship of the one God and his Son, of the previously divided peoples of the world. Revelation envisages the result of Jesus' victory in terms of a huge gathering, from every nation and tribe and people and language, all singing and shouting at the tops of their voices in praise of God and the Lamb.[40] Something has happened to break the divisive grip of the 'powers'. The early Christians declare that what had happened was the death of Jesus – the victory, as in Isaiah 40 – 55, of the covenant love of the Creator God in person, sharing and bearing the sins of his people and the world. By taking the people's sins, Jesus has robbed the 'powers' of their regular means of usurping human authority, freeing up humans of all sorts to become at last what they were made to be: worshippers of the one God, exercising royal priesthood in his world.[41]

That is why, perhaps to our surprise, the 'powers' are *reconciled*. Colossians 2:13–15 is the missing link, as it were, between 1:15–16 and 1:18b–20. Created; *defeated*; and then reconciled. The fact that

---

40 Revelation 7:9–12.

41 For more on the victory of the cross, see Wright, *The Day the Revolution Began*.

God has celebrated his triumph over the rebel powers doesn't mean that there is no role for 'powers' any more. It is easy for modern Western observers, instantly suspicious of all 'powers', to be glad that the 'powers' were 'defeated' and then to leave it at that, content with a sneering critique of all human authorities. Such a perspective might seem to imply that perhaps a cheerful anarchy, or a kind of optimistic 'people's republic' with no visible power structures, would solve the problems of a city, a nation or the world. On the contrary: just as humans, liberated from sin, can take their rightful place as the royal priesthood, so the structures of governance, the tendons and ligaments of complex human society, are in principle *reconciled*. God intends that humans should share in running his world, and should be held accountable. Structures through which this happens – though still vulnerable to abuse and distortion – are not automatically evil. On the contrary, they are thus in principle reaffirmed and celebrated. As with everything else in God's creation, once they stop being worshipped they stop being demonic. It takes the victory of the cross to break their power. But, once that has happened, wise humans can and must rise to the challenge of establishing and maintaining God's intention for a well-functioning human society. We recognise, of course, that all our present efforts will fall short of the ideal, but we cannot for that reason shirk the attempt. Here as elsewhere we must avoid any facile over-realised eschatology, whether it be in the form of an unquestioned 'divine right of kings' or in the form of an equally unquestioned *vox populi, vox Dei*. Kings can err. So can mobs. So, too, can democratically elected majorities. That is why wise critique – a central part of the Church's vocation – remains vital.

The new vision for Church and world

Returning to the New Testament, we must make a point which, though obvious at one level, might well be overlooked. John and Paul (and for that matter Luke, Mark, the author of Revelation and all the others) assume that what had just been achieved through the death and resurrection of Jesus was (1) the fulfilment of Israel's

Scriptures and therefore (2) for the benefit of the whole world, Jew and Gentile alike, just as the Psalms and Isaiah had repeatedly insisted. They did not, in other words, *translate* the biblical promises into another dimension: say, that of Plato. They did not say, 'Well, Scripture promised a renewal of Jerusalem, but we now see that this means the "heavenly Jerusalem".' They had no thought that the reconciliation and new creation spoken of in the Psalms and Isaiah now turned out to be referring to the 'heavenly salvation' of people's 'souls'. In Revelation, after all, the 'new Jerusalem' comes *down* from heaven to earth, rather than inviting 'souls' to go *up* to reach it.[42] So what had changed with the coming of Israel's Messiah?

The radical transformation that took place through the events concerning Jesus had three related elements. First, it had to do with the long-prophesied change of focus from the Jewish people and their homeland to the worldwide Jew-plus-Gentile family, including the various social adjustments required if that was to work, as we see for instance in Romans 14. Second, it had to do with the liberating sense that new creation was now possible, in a way it had not been before, because in the Messiah's death and resurrection, and the gift of his own spirit to his followers, the victory had been won which opened the way for advance signs of God's new world to come to birth, not least precisely in the formation of believing communities made up of people of every kind. Third, it introduced the radical idea, glimpsed in Isaiah's 'servant' figure, that both the ultimate victory and the manner of its implementation would consist not in violence but in suffering love. These three clearly belong together.

Thus one of the most striking moments in Paul's letter to the Romans, often ignored because it comes near the end of a long and demanding epistle, is the quotation of Isaiah 11:10 with which Paul

---

42 On Paul's use of the 'heavenly Jerusalem' in Galatians 4:26, see Wright, *Galatians*, pp. 298–305. For a brief critique of the 'beatific vision' theory of e.g. Hans Boersma, see N. T. Wright, 'The Vision of God and the Kingdom of God: Theological and ecumenical reflections', in *Rhetoric, History and Theology: Interpreting the New Testament*, ed. T. D. Still and J. A. Myers (Lanham, MD: Lexington/Fortress Academic, 2022), pp. 257–73.

triumphantly rounds off his argument in Romans 15:7–13.[43] When Jews and Gentiles – people of all sorts and conditions – learn to worship God the Creator with one heart and voice, they not only fulfil the Scriptures that spoke of this coming day. They embody in advance the prophetically promised new creation in which the wolf and the lamb will lie down together, living at peace under the wise and healing justice of the Messiah. Isaiah 11:1–10 as a whole stands behind Paul's entire argument, making a circle with the Scripture-fulfilling messianic statement at the start of the letter.[44] And this is why Paul closes that paragraph by invoking the blessing of 'the God of hope'. The *present* multicultural family of believers, created by the gospel and sustained by the spirit, is the real and tangible sign in the present time of the ultimate renewal of all creation promised in Romans 8:18–30. The present 'filling' with hope (Romans 15:13) is the anticipation of the time promised in Isaiah 11:9 when the whole earth shall be 'filled' with the knowledge of YHWH as the waters cover the sea. Paul has not abandoned the very much this-worldly hope of Israel's Scriptures. He has shown, in a detail which not all his readers have followed, how that biblical hope is to be fulfilled at last, and how that eventual fulfilling is to be anticipated even in the present time.

The young church found itself in an unexpected position vis-à-vis the actual powers of the first-century world. We watch in awe as the early apostles, and then Paul, navigate their way through uncharted waters, with Peter and the others telling the Sanhedrin that they had to obey God rather than human authorities, and Paul appearing to take delight in telling both the Philippian magistrates and the high priest himself how to do their jobs. We should be clear: they were not saying, in effect, that human authorities were unimportant, irrelevant or to be abolished forthwith. They were calling them to account, informing or reminding them of

---

43 On what follows, see more fully in N. T. Wright, 'The Sign of New Creation: Romans 15.7–13', in *It's About Life: The formative power of Scripture*, ed. J. Coutts et al. (Vancouver: Regent Publications, 2023), pp. 219–37.

44 Romans 1:3–5.

their God-given role in the Creator's world. They were, in fact, doing what Jesus said in the farewell discourses:

> When [the spirit] comes, he will prove the world to be in the wrong on three counts: sin, justice and judgement. In relation to sin – because they don't believe in me. In relation to justice – because I'm going to the father, and you won't see me anymore. In relation to judgement – because the ruler of this world is judged.[45]

This is itself a matter of *inaugurated eschatology*. The divine judgement which will hold all rulers and authorities to account in the end is *anticipated* in the spirit-driven witness of the Church to those same authorities in the present time. This is cognate with Paul's (to us) strange throwaway line to the effect that, since Jesus' followers will one day find themselves judging angels, they ought to be able, already, to make wise judgements relating to their present community.[46] In other words, it is a central part of the Church's task, in the power and leading of the spirit, to hold up a mirror to worldly power, to hold authorities to account. In terms of Colossians, this vocation *implements* the 'defeat' of the powers and then *invites* their 'reconciliation'. I think of Paul challenging Herod Agrippa II as to whether he believed the prophets, and if so whether he ought not to be open to the possibility that Jesus of Nazareth really had been raised from the dead.[47] (In our world, interestingly, the news media assume that the task of holding authorities to account belongs to them, often thereby setting themselves up as a new kind of 'authority'. They thus, having taken over the Church's vocation, regularly delight both in reporting the Church's follies and failings – of which there have tragically been many – and in downgrading Christian practice to the status of a curious minority hobby, which is of course how many Christians appear to understand their faith).

---

45 John 16:8–11.
46 1 Corinthians 6:2–3.
47 Acts 26:26–9.

On speaking truth to power

We should note that for the early Christians, as indeed for Jews of the period, the critique of worldly powers had nothing to do with how the present rulers had attained their position. People became rulers through conquest, wealth, murder, inheritance, appointment by some other power (Herod the Great was nominated as 'king of the Jews' by Augustus simply because he was the most successful local warlord), and in many other ways. How they got there was not the point. The modern Western democratic ideal, in which the winner of an election receives political power that goes unchallenged because the people have voted for it, would have made little sense. The early Christians, like the Jews, focused their critique not on *how the rulers had become rulers* but on *what the rulers then did* with the power they now had.

The idea of speaking the truth to power was not new. It was central to the prophetic vocation. It is what Nathan did to David. It is what Daniel and his friends had done in the court of Babylon. But it comes now, for the early Christians, with a fresh sense of possibility, and of a vocation much wider than that of occasional heroic figures. God wants his world to be properly run, but the standard for 'properly' is that of Psalm 72: the wise, healing justice of the Messiah's rule, caring for the poor and needy, confronting and overthrowing the bullies and the oppressors, opening the way for the whole world to be filled with God's glory. Where that is not happening, the Messiah's people are commissioned, and equipped by the spirit, to point out the failure and urge people, as Jesus and his first followers did, to repent and amend their ways. There is plenty of evidence that church leaders in the second and third century did exactly this, challenging rulers and authorities (for instance) about the plight of the poor.[48] And there is plenty of evidence that, in their common life, the 'ordinary' Jesus-followers of those centuries lived in such a way as, by their sheer example, to hold wider society to account

---

48 See, for instance, R. Stark, *The Rise of Christianity: A sociologist reconsiders history* (Princeton, NJ: Princeton University Press, 1996).

in respect of its idolatry and the dehumanising practices which followed, for instance in relation to the exposure of unwanted infants.

This remains true whether or not the Church appeared to 'succeed'. In a way, martyrdom itself proves the same point, of the arrival on the scene of a new kind of human life, the Jesus-shaped way of wise and healing justice, in the face of which death had lost its ultimate power. New creation is demonstrated by faithfulness unto death just as much as by calling the 'powers' to account in word and example.

Why has this vision, of holding the world to account, not been eagerly embraced by followers of Jesus? At one level, the answer is obvious: it is challenging, difficult and quite possibly dangerous, as it was for Paul and his churches. (Among the difficulties we might note the problem of discernment: how to tell when the Church is simply following some local fad or fashion.) But at another level – and this brings us with a flying leap into our own era – the Church has often remained unaware of this aspect of its calling. There are many Christians today, not least in the modern Western world, who have no idea that the Jesus whom they worship did indeed win the victory over the dark powers of the world, let alone what that might mean in practice. And this has left the door open for very different, and unbiblical, visions of the political calling of the followers of Jesus. As in earlier days, when it was possible for devout Christians to imagine that a bloodthirsty 'crusade' might be God's will, so today many are simply, and sometimes dangerously, confused. Some opt for an escapist piety in the present and a distant 'heaven' in the future, leaving the present world untouched lest they get embroiled in its messy ways. Others enlist clergy to bless their bombs and their bullets. How did we get here, and how do we get back on track?

God's purposes through God's people in a political world

For a start, from at least the third century onwards, it became increasingly common for Christian thinkers to blend together elements of the biblical message with the newer versions of Plato's philosophy that were becoming popular. We have already considered the misunderstandings around the 'heavenly Jerusalem'. For the Neoplatonist, the aim was not for a multi-ethnic and multilingual community to worship together as the sign of hope in the present, pointing towards what the Creator God would eventually do for the whole cosmos. The aim was for the individual 'soul' to be so purified that, after death, it would leave the world of space, time and matter and make its way into the divine presence in 'heaven'.

It cannot be stressed too strongly that none of this is found in the New Testament.[49] It represents a major step away from the biblical vision to which Jesus and his first followers were obedient. (This is why, of course, from the third century onwards, methods of reading Scripture were developed to make the Bible address what people thought it *ought* to be addressing – a process that continues to our own day.) As long as people are focused on 'going to heaven', they will have less compulsion to pursue the New Testament's vision of a united trans-ethnic and trans-local family worshipping the one God *and thus holding the powers of the world to account*. Indeed, they may warn that this is all too 'worldly', a distraction from a proper 'heavenly' focus. Thus the Church's vocation to speak truth to power, the truth of God's wise, healing justice, sustained by the knowledge that the powers of the world have actually been defeated on the cross, can easily go by the board when people 'translate' the language of Jesus' victory into the message of 'going to heaven' despite ongoing sin. Of course sin, forgiveness, reconciliation with God and with one another, continue to matter. But for the first Christians, these were realities to be worked out in actual community, not simply private transactions between God and the soul. Sin continues to matter because it is the fruit of idolatry; if left unforgiven and unchecked, it will lead to death, to the collapse of the image-bearing vocation. This ultimate sad future is anticipated if

---

49 An obvious example: when Matthew has Jesus speak of 'the kingdom of heaven', this refers, not to a place called 'heaven' to which Jesus' followers will eventually go (as most modern readers imagine), but to the rule of 'heaven' in God's coming new age 'on earth as in heaven'. Why, otherwise, would Jesus (like the psalmist) promise the meek that they would inherit the earth (Matthew 5:5; Psalm 37:11)?

and when the Church or part of the Church, having become trapped in idolatry, cannot then hold the idolatrous powers to account. An older form of Christian teaching warned that sinning risked a post-mortem hell. The biblical warnings assume that hell already exists for many people here on earth, and that it is the Church's task both to analyse and denounce the idolatries that produce it and to model the way of life that, through the spirit, reflects instead the image of the true God revealed in Jesus. This will form the anticipation, however partial, of the promised and prayed-for hope 'on earth as in heaven'. That, indeed, is what Paul goes on to say in Colossians. Here again the emphasis is on the new kind of family in which (following the defeat of the 'powers') people of all classes and ethnicities are welcome on equal terms:

> You have put on the new [human nature] – which is being renewed in the image of the creator, bringing you into possession of new knowledge. In this humanity there is no question of 'Greek and Jew,' or 'circumcised or uncircumcised,' of 'barbarian, Scythian,' or 'slave and free.' The Messiah is everything and in everything![50]

The very existence of a community living like that – scandalous as it appeared to many – was the sign to the watching world that something radically new had come about, a way of life that was attractive and vibrant even as, in social and political terms, it was costly and dangerous. To read on in Colossians 3 is to be struck by what amounts to a miniature version of the Sermon on the Mount: a blueprint for a new-creation people, demonstrating before the world what a genuinely human community should look like:

> You must be tender-hearted, kind, humble, meek, and ready to put up with anything. You must bear with one another and, if anyone has a complaint against someone else, you must forgive each other . . . On top of all this you must put on love,

---

50 Colossians 3:10–11. Compare the similar passage in Galatians 3:27–9.

which ties everything together and makes it complete. Let the Messiah's peace be the deciding factor in your hearts; that's what you were called to, within the one body. And be thankful. Let the Messiah's word dwell richly among you, as you teach and exhort one another in all wisdom, singing psalms, hymns and spiritual songs to God with grateful hearts. And whatever you do, in word or action, do everything in the name of the master, Jesus, giving thanks through him to God the father.[51]

These are the virtues and practices of the community for whom Jesus has become the centre of life. Once we start pondering what this way of life really means, we have, in effect, a whole political vision, including economy, the environment, community development and plenty more. A community like this will not simply respect existing structures: it will be reshaping them from within. Reflecting God's image to the world around is more than simply offering an alternative vision. It can and should be transformative.[52]

Alas, there is a lot of ground to make up. The concentration of the Church, for much of its history, on the unbiblical theme of 'going to heaven', instead of on Jesus' priority of God's kingdom coming 'on earth as in heaven', has opened the door to multiple misunderstandings, the results of which are all around us today. This plays out in many areas of church life, but the political fallout is perhaps the most dangerous. In the sixteenth century, the Protestant Reformers were eager (rightly in my view) to have the Bible and public worship in language understood by ordinary people. But they seem to have ignored the biblical imperative – going back to Pentecost itself, and coming forward to that multi-lingual celebration in Revelation 7 and Romans 15 – to bring different nations and languages *together* in the worship of God. Thus, already by the seventeenth century, many European cities contained worshipping communities divided along linguistic lines: English-speaking

---

51 Colossians 3:12–17.
52 For more on this see Brian J. Walsh and Sylvia C. Keesmaat, *Colossians Remixed: Subverting the empire* (Downers Grove, IL: InterVarsity Press, 2004), ch. 10.

churches, French-speaking churches, Spanish, Germanic and a host of others. And by the twentieth century, many of these had developed different theological emphases . . . which, both in their countries of origin and when transported to the colonies in the 'new world', went on to establish themselves as rival orthodoxies. And because the emphasis was on enabling people to 'go to heaven', nobody seems to have noticed that the New Testament itself constantly stressed that it was the cross-cultural unity of the Church that would hold the powers to account. In Paul's striking vision in Ephesians, the purpose of God to bring together in the Messiah all things in heaven and earth (1:10) was to be displayed in advance through the coming together of Jew and Gentile in the Church (2:11–22), with the result that 'God's wisdom, in all its rich variety, was to be made known to the rulers and authorities in the heavenly places – through the church!'[53] Not much chance, one might think, of that today.

Jesus and the hope for the nations

It is perhaps not surprising that Ephesians and Colossians were regarded by some liberal Protestant scholars in nineteenth-century Germany as non-Pauline. It wasn't just that the 'high Christology', or even the 'high ecclesiology', of these two letters was unwelcome to many, though it was. Ephesians and Colossians, fully in line with Romans and Galatians, only perhaps more explicitly, were articulating a view of the Church's identity and responsibility in relation to the 'powers'. But in nineteenth-century Europe, as indeed in north America, 'nation states' were inventing themselves as a new sort of 'power', with anthems and flags and a sense of individual 'identity' and even, in some cases, 'destiny'. Perhaps even a 'God-given' or 'manifest' destiny. Because the churches in many countries had focused their teaching on an otherworldly piety and salvation, this might not have seemed to matter. But many such countries had strong Christian traditions woven into their national

---

53 Ephesians 3:10.

life which could be brought on board in support of the new national agenda. It was not only some of the American founding fathers who thought of themselves as the 'new Israel' discovering the 'promised land'. Some French Canadians saw the province of Quebec in the same way. It became fatally easy to suppose, as many in Europe, not least Britain, had done before, that this or that country was automatically 'Christian', and that whatever it needed to do in pursuit of its national identity and destiny would somehow be underwritten by that 'religious' label.

There is an important paradox here. 'Religion', after all, had been redefined through the philosophy of the Enlightenment. In the ancient world, worship of the gods was woven into every aspect of ordinary living; but, in post-Enlightenment Europe and America, 'religion' was *by definition* separated off from everything else.[54] Having been thereby emasculated in terms of the possibility of political *critique* (that of course did continue in specific areas, as in the campaigns against slavery, but in wider terms it had ceased to matter), 'religion', such as it had become, could easily be co-opted in favour of specific national aspirations. Thus the *Deutsche Christen* were an important part of Hitler's programme, just as ninety years later the idea of 'Holy Russia' has been invoked in support of Putin's war against Ukraine.[55] The British, once again, are hardly innocent on this score, to say the least. It all reminds me uncomfortably of the moment when the Israelites, suffering defeat at the hands of the Philistines, had the bright idea of bringing the ark of the covenant into the line of battle.[56]

This kind of 'Christian nationalism' is, as it were, an ideological accident waiting to happen. It presents a standing temptation, whenever the on-earth-as-in-heaven message of the New Testament has been sidelined in favour of the supposedly 'spiritual' teaching

---

54 On this shift, see Brent Nongbri, *Before Religion: A history of a modern concept* (New Haven, CT: Yale University Press, 2013); and Wright, *History and Eschatology*, ch. 1.

55 See Katherine Kelaidis, *Holy Russia? Holy War? Why the Russian Church is backing Putin against Ukraine* (London: SPCK, 2023).

56 1 Samuel 4:1–22.

Power and the 'Powers' in Early Christianity

of 'going to heaven', either in the ascent of the soul after death or in a 'rapture' at the Lord's return.[57]

The result is clear: the 'powers' are still dictating the terms. You can always tell. Idols demand sacrifices; the sacrifices are often human. Jesus said, after all, that the difference between his kingdom, which was not 'from this world', and those kingdoms that *were* 'from this world' was that if his kingdom had been of the ordinary kind then his followers would fight.[58] When a supposed 'Christian nationalism' goes hand in hand with a culture that glorifies violence, and the means of violence, at whatever level; where the churches are so divided that they have no collective witness with which to speak the truth to the powers in question; where people ignore the regular biblical insistence on the love of enemies, and the goal of a single multi-ethnic worshipping community, and prefer de facto ethnically based separate assemblies; where truth ceases to matter, either because it is deconstructed into 'my truth' and 'your truth' or because political leaders so obviously tell lies – then the gospel, the *euangelion*, is being denied, irrespective of how many people within 'the system' think of themselves as *evangelisch* or 'evangelical'. Jesus warned against mistaking the work of God's holy spirit for the work of the devil. There is equal danger the other way round, when people suppose they are working for God while unthinkingly serving the 'powers'.[59]

Thus the ambiguities of power in the Old Testament are echoed, though in a different mode, in the life of the Church. This isn't simply a repetition of old mistakes, though it can sometimes look like that. Would-be 'Christian monarchs' can abuse their position. So can elected officials, if – for instance – they brandish a Bible in the hopes of recruiting the support of the devout for their unbiblical

---

57 For the critique of the 'rapture' theory, see N. T. Wright, *Surprised by Hope: Rethinking heaven, the resurrection and the mission of the Church* (London: SPCK, 2007), ch. 8; and Bird, *Evangelical Theology*, pp. 346–50.

58 John 18:36. As discussed above, Jesus' saying has often been misunderstood to mean that his kingdom was 'otherworldly' in the sense of being only 'in heaven'. The Greek is clear: Jesus' kingdom does not *originate in* this world, but it is emphatically designed *for* this world.

59 Matthew 12:32; cf. John 16:2.

71

actions and attitudes. Just because Jesus' death, resurrection and ascension to world sovereignty have brought about a radically new situation, that does not mean (alas) that his followers will not get things badly wrong – as the book of Acts already indicates. The study of church history highlights so many shameful episodes – persecution of non-Christians, Crusades, Inquisitions, holy (and bloody) revolutions, and so on – that it is easy to forget that, alongside these very visible wickednesses, there have been millions of ordinary believers who have lived out, as best they could, the Sermon on the Mount. And it is they who, through meekness, mourning, purity of heart and hunger for justice, have carried forward the flame of the gospel. For every high-profile would-be 'Christian' leader who has led all-too-willing followers into a battle based on lies, arrogance, greed and the lust for power, there are (thank God) countless unsung heroines and heroes who have heeded the words of Jesus about those who want to be leaders needing to be the servant of all.

Between Coronation and New Creation

All this brings us back to the Coronation of Charles III. Debates continue to rumble on, in the UK and elsewhere, about the appropriateness of constitutional monarchy in a post-Enlightenment world. That is a whole other question. But it was noticeable that, even before the Prime Minister read the striking passage from Colossians with which we began, the new king himself had quoted Jesus' own words about having come not to be served but to serve. Whether or not he lives up to that statement, and whether or not other leaders in the UK or elsewhere take note and follow suit, it was at least a good way to begin.

After all, a good deal of the New Testament, following directly from the teaching and example of Jesus himself, is about the radical redefinition of power: power in weakness, power through humble service, power and indeed victory through self-sacrifice. It is the crucified and risen Jesus who declares to his followers that 'all authority in heaven and on earth has been given to me'.[60] We have a sense that the Church, for much of its history, has been quite happy to think of Jesus having all authority in heaven, but has yet to work out what it might mean that he – the Jesus of cross, resurrection and spirit – already possesses all authority on earth. A good way to begin that discussion might be with Psalm 72, which emphasises that the priorities of God's true King are looking after the poor and needy and rescuing them from oppression and violence. The reconciled 'powers' – the structures of a wise society, working together as true human beings to reflect the loving, healing wisdom and justice of the Creator God – need constantly to be recalled to this vision. And the Church, in articulating that call, must constantly be on the alert lest, having preached to others, it might itself fail in its own version of the same task. The Church's mission today is to be ambassadors of reconciliation, speaking truth to power, and seeing the powers reconciled to God. That does not collapse future hopes into present endeavours, but it does mean that our earthly labours are signs pointing ahead to a renewed creation. Our mission is not to be the 'religious department' of an empire. It is, rather, to build for the kingdom. How do we do that? What might it look like?

---

60 Matthew 28:18.

73

4

The Kingdom of God as Vision and Vocation

A tale of two British prime ministers

There was one particularly famous incident during Tony Blair's tenure as British prime minister (1997–2007) when he was asked by a *Vanity Fair* journalist about his faith. Before Blair could answer, Alastair Campbell, his media advisor, blurted out that 'Downing Street doesn't do God'. Blair himself had made no secret of his Christian faith. After leaving public office, he would even be received into the Roman Catholic Church. But there was a sense in which Campbell's remark was true. PM Blair, for all his faith, did not regularly consult or engage with faith leaders on the pressing questions of the late 1990s and early 2000s. Blair is certainly a man of genuine faith, but his faith while in office was compartmentalised, siloed away from the rest of his political vision. He did not 'do God' in the sense of integrating his Christian faith into his political vision, one that appeared to sway from cynical pragmatism to neo-liberal idealism.

To be fair to Blair, he is hardly alone in that failure. Ever since the Enlightenment, God, religion and the Church have been removed into the private sphere, like a demented elderly relative confined to the upstairs attic: we can visit him from time to time, but he mustn't be allowed to come downstairs and embarrass us, especially when there are visitors present. To say that one does not 'do God' in public policy means to disregard religious considerations even when considering all things. It means telling the Church to mind its own business and not to stick its nose where it is not wanted, even if it might have some valid things to say about a given topic. It is a recipe for a two-storey universe in which God dwells 'up there' and God has little to do with anything 'down here'.

The strange thing is that we find the exact opposite view given by another British prime minister, David Cameron (2010–16). Cameron claimed to be 'evangelical' about his faith, wanting to see a bigger role for religion in the UK, respecting its Christian heritage, and he urged his fellow believers to be more confident in promoting their Christian views.[1] Cameron could even criticise the Church of England for its woolliness and fuzziness when it came to stating its beliefs precisely. Yet Cameron was frustrated when the Church of England failed to approve the appointment of women bishops in 2015. In response, he said that he would certainly examine how the British Parliament could compel the Church – note these words – 'to get with the programme' when it came to gender equality in the Church.

We believe in the ordination of women into the episcopate, and it has since transpired, but were equally appalled by Cameron's nakedly interventionist views. Cameron's threat of political interference in the Church's internal affairs smacked of straightforward 'Erastianism', a view in which the State rules supreme over the Church even to the extent of dictating religious matters. For the Church to get with any programme is a seductive desire it must always resist. The spirit of the age is in any case notoriously fickle. You might as well be walking in the mist and taking a compass bearing on a mountain goat. What is more, it is worth remembering too that sometimes the Church must reluctantly say to the civil authorities 'we must obey God, not human beings'.[2] The Church does not exist to provide religious sponsorship to anyone's programmes.

---

1   Rowena Mason, 'David Cameron: I Am Evangelical about Christian Faith', *The Guardian*, 17 April 2014: https://www.theguardian.com/politics/2014/apr/16/david-cameron-evangelical-about-christian-faith (accessed 18 August 2023).

2   Acts 5:29; and Acts 4:19, 'But Peter and John gave them this reply: "You judge," they said, "whether it's right before God to listen to you rather than to God!"'

It is odd that Blair and Cameron represent opposite responses about the place of the Church in the political realm. The Church and its message is either exiled to the attic of heavenly-mindedness, or else it is made a servant of the State to be bossed around at the will and whim of a leader. We want to suggest that Blair and Cameron were prime examples of what happens when a Christian politician doesn't think through a serious Christian political theology.

The fact is that all Christians, whether as private citizens or as public figures, must be willing to 'do God' in public. We must be concerned with the entailments of the gospel for ourselves, for our churches, for our cities and for our world. Oliver O'Donovan puts it well:

> Theology must be political if it is to be evangelical. Rule out the political questions and you cut short the proclamation of God's saving power; you leave people enslaved where they ought to be set free from sin – their own sin and others'.[3]

There is no opt-out for us if we are committed to Jesus as Lord and the way that lordship becomes part of a life lived in community with others. To be clear, this is not about a Christian takeover. It is about Christian testimony in an age of troubles, terror, tyranny and tragedy. The reason for that is simple: the kingdom of God. Precisely because we believe that Jesus is King and his kingly power is operative among us, we cannot retreat to the attic of spiritual affairs, not when there is a gospel to proclaim and a hurting world crying out for healing and hope. Precisely because Jesus is the King of kings, we offer him our worship and allegiance, while earthly monarchs and ministers of state may expect from us our intercession, taxes, counsel and service, a service that in its own way advances God's purposes for human affairs.

Aristotle said that humans are a 'political animal' in that they are social creatures and want to order their civic lives for some

---

3   Oliver O'Donovan, *The Desire of the Nations: Rediscovering the roots of political theology* (Cambridge: Cambridge University Press, 1996), p. 3.

good end. The Bible has an analogous thought, except that instead of 'political animal' we have the 'image of God', which is the human vocation for reflecting God's sovereign rule over creation, and the good end for which we aim, and towards which we orientate ourselves, is the 'new heaven and new earth'.[4] That human vocation is not abandoned by Jesus and his church; rather, they are meant to be the agents for its penultimate and ultimate manifestation. The redeeming of human institutions such as government, the curation of creation, making them good, making them fit for their divinely called purposes – this prepares for the kingdom, ahead of the ultimate unveiling of God the Father's rule in Jesus with his church: when 'everything is put in order under' Jesus and 'we [the Church] shall reign with him' over a healed and holy world.[5] Jesus' followers build for that kingdom with public activism and service. If so, then, 'political responsibility in this age', comments James Skillen, 'does not belong to a kingdom separate from Christ's kingdom but is one of the modes of service that humans everywhere owe to God and their neighbors in the one and only kingdom of God that is not yet fully disclosed'.[6]

Accordingly, we must 'do God'; we must be involved, active and activist, in public, in politics, in matters for which our kingdom-calling requires us. Christians might be safe hiding and huddled together in the catacombs for fear of being seduced by political power, but that is not how discipleship works. We must live luminously visible lives that appear odd to others because of our allegiance to Jesus and adopting a life patterned after Jesus. Christians are not distinguished from others by language, food, dress or convention, but by their 'peculiar way of life' and the 'strange character of their own citizenship'.[7] Abbreviate those differences as faith, love, hope and virtue if you like, but they are exercised in the public square and for the sake of the world. Augustine understood that the 'city of God' was not

---

4   Genesis 1:27–8; Revelation 21:1.

5   1 Corinthians 15:28; 2 Timothy 2:12.

6   James W. Skillen, *The Good of Politics: A biblical, historical, and contemporary introduction* (Grand Rapids, MI: Baker, 2014), p. 34.

7   *Epistle to Diognetus* 5.2, 4 (trans. R. Brannan); cf. Augustine, *City of God* 19.19.

spatially separate from the 'earthly city', because the city of God was not a place but a pilgrimage within this world. A pilgrim may make use of temporal goods such as government, employing them for their divinely intended ends, without worshipping them and without being corrupted by idolatries of power.[8] If heavenly citizens do that, they will then be walking signposts of heavenly peace amid earthly chaos, and become a life-giving force in the world as a soul is to the body.[9]

Yet exercising public discipleship is fraught with risks. First up, Christians must resist any attempt to be co-opted or coerced by the State into practices that depart from our internal consensus and do not pass muster with biblical reasoning and creedal formulations. Similarly, we must have the courage to pursue our own consciences and convictions, not glibly attach ourselves to the visions of either the neo-conservative right or the radical left. We are to live faithfully within the symbols, story and message of King Jesus that bid us to clasp our hands in prayer as much as to put them to the trowel of earthly labour in his name. So how do we build for the kingdom without falling into the trap of spiritual isolationism or being led into captivity to a political master?

Revisiting the problem of cross and kingdom

An immediate point for us to grapple with is how we integrate our deep convictions about the Lord Jesus with the life of faith we are called to pursue in his name. When Tom Wright was bishop of Durham, he served a diocese that was in many ways a microcosm of the theological diversity in the Church of England, where parishes struggled to get the balance right in terms of their evangelical convictions and earnest energies for justice.

On the one hand, there were some churches in the diocese that were proudly Reformed in their preaching. These churches were steadfastly committed to the authority of Scripture, savoured the

---

8 Augustine, *City of God* 19.17.
9 Again, note the shared sentiments on this in the *Epistle to Diognetus* 6.1 and in Augustine, *City of God* 19.17, 20.

doctrines of grace, and faithfully proclaimed the message of the cross. For in that message, they rightly saw the heart of the gospel: the atonement, justification by faith, and Jesus giving himself as a sacrifice for us. They loved Paul's epistles, but found it harder to discern the same package in the Gospels. It was almost as if Jesus, his kingdom-message and healings, were just the warm-up to Paul's letters. In fact, as long as Jesus was born of a virgin and died on the cross, he could have lived in Swansea or New Jersey for all it mattered, and in any period of history. Jesus was just a divine prop for Paul's message of the cross. What that had to do with the kingdom was a bit of a mystery.

On the other hand, other churches in the diocese were committed to Jesus' kingdom as a message and way of life. For them, discipleship meant the imitation of Jesus, living out the parables of Jesus, praying for the sick, cultivating compassion and assisting those in poverty. As they read the Gospels, they saw Jesus as a pioneer of social justice, to the point where some even thought that it was such a shame he was crucified so young, because he was on quite a roll. Such churches were very comfortable with the Gospels, but struggled with the Pauline epistles and the letter to the Hebrews. Surely Jesus was a champion of the marginalised and oppressed, and that's where the Church should be now. The fixation on his crucifixion, death and paying our moral debts all sounded too macabre or medieval to them.

As you can tell, both types of churches latched on to something quite right, genuinely true, and authentically Christian. But they had pulled apart what belonged together, the **cross** and the **kingdom**. The result was a series of unhelpful dichotomies: the atonement or healing, crucifixion or crown, God's forgiveness or God's transformative love.

The problem is not merely that well-meaning people are sometimes unaware of how Jesus' cross and God's kingdom sit together. It is far more than that: they do not understand that cross and kingdom do not make sense without each other.[10] Grasping this is vital

---

10 See more fully N. T. Wright, *How God Became King: Getting to the heart of the Gospels* (London: SPCK, 2012), with mention in dispatches for Jeremy R. Treat, *The Crucified King: Atonement and kingdom in biblical and systematic theology* (Grand Rapids, MI: Zondervan, 2014).

for a proper theological understanding of Christian mission. For only after we have understood how the cross and the kingdom go together will we be equipped to consider how Christians carry with them the marks of Jesus' death and the message of Jesus' kingdom. We can't be content with being either a cross-centred church or a kingdom-centred church. We must have both, otherwise preaching will be impoverished, and our faith will lack deeds infused with Jesus' kingdom-ministry. That's why we need a regular diet of the Gospels in the Church's life. The Gospels tell the story of God becoming King, in King Jesus, and the crucifixion is the centrepiece in that story.

The story the Evangelists all tell brings together beautifully these two major themes of cross and kingdom. They are telling the story of how the deeds, suffering, death and resurrection of Israel's Messiah somehow bring about his worldwide sovereign kingdom. In that kingdom, there is reconciliation, forgiveness, liberation and justice. Not just justice declared over us, but justice about us, in us and for us.

Centuries of atonement theology explored the manifold ways in which we might say that Jesus' death delivers us from our sins. But this was siloed away from the advent of God's own kingly power in Jesus and dislocated from God's exaltation of Jesus as 'Lord' and 'Messiah'. That, perhaps, is why traditional atonement-theologies have, bizarrely to my mind, failed to draw on the Gospels for their primary source material, save only the ransom saying of Matthew 20:28 and Mark 10:45.[11] But even in those two texts, we do well to remember that it is the 'son of man' who serves and redeems, the son of man as Israel's supreme representative, a job description for Isaiah's suffering Servant.[12] Jesus' self-description implied that he was the righteous sufferer, the one who enters the deathly hallows, who gives his life as a ransom for others and is somehow rescued

---

11 'That's how it is with the son of man: he didn't come to have servants obey him, but to *be* a servant – and to give his life as "a ransom for many"' (Matthew 20:28) and 'Don't you see? The son of man didn't come to be waited on. He came to be the servant, to give his life "as a ransom for many"' (Mark 10:45).

12 Isaiah 52 – 53.

into the light of life. This happens not only for his own sake, but so that God's 'kingdom' breaks in and breaks through, and so that God's own people share in his victory and dominion.

Again, conversely, traditional kingdom-theologies, with an emphasis on God's liberation of the oppressed, have regularly held aloof from speaking too much about the cross. Yet people have strangely missed something that the Evangelists make notoriously obvious. Jesus proclaims and enacts the 'kingdom of God', yet what we find in the *titulus* over the cross at the climax of the story is the naked proclamation of the kingship of the crucified.[13] Pilate's cruel, mocking jibe, 'This is Jesus, the King of the Jews', no doubt intended to strike terror into the mind of any would-be royal aspirant, turns out to be communicating a stunning truth. This is how the kingdom comes. This is the kingdom of God in power, this is God's saving reign, this is Israel's King saving his people.[14]

In all four Gospels, then, there is no dumbing this down: this is the coming of the kingdom, the sovereign rule of Israel's God arriving on earth as in heaven, exercised through David's true son and heir, the 'Messiah'. The kingdom comes through his death. The fact that the kingdom is redefined by the cross doesn't mean that it isn't still the kingdom. The fact that the cross is the kingdom-bringing event doesn't mean that it isn't still an act of horrible and brutal injustice on the one hand, and powerful, rescuing divine love on the other. The two meanings are brought into dramatic, shocking but permanent relation. Ultimately, the cross *is* the sharp edge of kingdom-redefinition, just as the kingdom, in its redefined form, *is* the ultimate meaning of the cross.

It is not hard to see how kingdom-proclamation and kingdom-praxis go together. Jesus told people to 'Repent!' because 'The kingdom of heaven is arriving!' and he specifically called Peter and Andrew to follow him so that they would now 'fish for people'.[15]

---

13 Matthew 27:36–7.

14 On the early Christian view of 'the kingdom come in power', see N. T. Wright, *History and Eschatology: Jesus and the promise of natural theology* (Waco, TX: Baylor University Press, 2019), ch. 4.

15 Matthew 4:17–19.

Jesus then went about Galilee, '*proclaiming* the good news of the kingdom, *healing* every disease and every illness among the people'.[16] His preaching, healings and exorcisms by the power of the spirit were the proof that 'God's kingdom has arrived on your doorstep'.[17] What is more, Peter would later proclaim the message of Jesus to the people of Jerusalem,[18] to Judaean rulers,[19] and to Gentiles such as Cornelius of Caesarea.[20] Peter's sermons were soaked in themes of scriptural fulfilment combined with summaries of Jesus' message and public career. They did not shrink from mentioning his gruesome death. They rejoiced in Jesus' resurrection and exaltation, climaxed in the call for repentance and baptism, and promised the forgiveness of sins and the gift of the holy spirit to everyone who responded in faith. At the same time, Peter also continued the public work of Jesus by healing a crippled beggar just as Jesus did;[21] Peter healed a paralytic man just as Jesus did;[22] Peter resuscitated a widow who had died just as Jesus did for a widow's son;[23] Peter gave testimony before the Jerusalem leaders just as Jesus did.[24]

The Church's message was abbreviated by Luke as announcing 'the message about God's kingdom and the Name of Jesus the Messiah'.[25] When that message is spoken, when that royal work is done, then there are people repenting and believing, many 'turning to the Lord'. In addition, there are baptisms, healings, deliverance from all sorts of oppression, calling out the injustices perpetrated against the innocent, and telling the powers that we must obey God, not human authorities. The Church is not the kingdom itself. The kingdom is the act of the one true God now ruling over the world in a new way through the healing victory of Jesus. People come to

16 Matthew 4:23, emphasis ours.
17 Matthew 12:28.
18 Acts 2:22–36; 3:12–26.
19 Acts 4:8–12.
20 Acts 10:34–46.
21 Mark 10:46–47; Acts 3:1–10.
22 Mark 2:1–12; Acts 9:32–35.
23 Luke 7:11–17; Acts 9:36–43.
24 Mark 14:53–65; Acts 4:1–21.
25 Acts 8:12.

belong within this new reality – being 'brought into the kingdom' in that sense – through the preaching, prayer and powerful healing work of Jesus' followers.

What is clearly *not* in mind is that preaching the cross to the 'lost' would happen in one church while acts of mercy for the poor would happen in another church. Advancing the kingdom means promoting the gospel from Jesus and about Jesus. Kingdom-work is continuing to do the very same things that Jesus himself did among individuals in need, challenging self-assured religious types, offering mercy to the downtrodden and forgotten, warning of judgement, exhorting faith in God's generous forgiveness, and speaking words of truth in the halls of political power. Jesus is the crucified and risen king who calls us to kingdom-allegiance and kingdom-deeds that are humbly cruciform and positively bursting with the life of the new creation.

The integration of cross and kingdom should cultivate a cross-shaped kingdom-perspective that flows into all theatres of life. The kingdom of God is the healing, rescuing sovereignty of the Creator God, working in the power of the spirit through the death and resurrection of Jesus to bring about the future consummation of heaven and earth. This ultimate future is anticipated in the present in the cruciform vocation of all Jesus' followers who, in their multiple different callings, are building for that kingdom here and now.

Building for the kingdom

Many people may have an allergic reaction to this language of 'building for the kingdom', with the kingdom as something that is advanced, embodied or even carried forward in our own vocation as followers of Jesus. It might sound a tad over-confident, as if we can, under our own steam, make the kingdom happen in the here and now. Some qualifications and clarifications may help.

First, God builds God's kingdom. The kingdom itself is not manufactured or constructed by human hands. Be that as it may, God has ordered his world in such a way that his own work within that world takes place precisely through his creatures, in particular, the human beings who reflect his image. That is central to what it means to be 'made in God's image'. God intends his wise, creative, loving presence and power to be reflected, 'imaged' if you like, into his world through his human creatures. God has enlisted us to act as his stewards in the project of creation and in new creation.

The notion of creaturely participation in divine rule is ingrained into the fabric of the scriptural story; it is part of the gospel, and is evoked in God's promises for the future. Adam's task in the garden was to be a king over creation and high priest of creation.[26] Even with the disaster of rebellion and corruption, God has still called human beings to be custodians of his creation. This is why the psalmist celebrates the fact that 'You have given them [humans] dominion over the works of your hands; you have put all things under their feet'.[27] That task of course reaches its climax in the exaltation of Jesus, because Jesus, even in (and precisely in!) his glorified state, retains his humanity, and it is as a human being, as true man and as true God, that he stands at the helm of the universe. No wonder Psalm 8 was applied to Jesus as the new Adam through whom God's reign is currently exercised.[28] But there's far more! What the new creation will look like, we are told by biblical authors, is that the Church will reign with Jesus in God's new world.[29] God has built into the gospel message the fact that, through the work of Jesus and the power of the spirit, he equips humans to help in the work of getting the creation project back on track and to share in its perfection in the coming age.

Thus, we have the calling of humanity to rule over creation on God's behalf, the exalted man Jesus as God the Father's co-regent in heaven right now, and the promise of the Church reigning with Jesus over the new creation. God's reign, then, clearly includes creaturely participation in divine rule, through humans. God's setting things right and making things new transpires through the exalted

---

26 Genesis 1:26–9.

27 Psalm 8:6.

28 See 1 Corinthians 15:27–8 and Hebrews 2:5–9.

29 See 2 Timothy 2:1 and Revelation 5:10; 22:5.

Jesus and his loyal subjects, both now and in the age to come. So the objection about our trying to build God's kingdom by our own efforts, though it seems humble and pious, can be a way of shirking our responsibility, of making nervous sideways glances when our master is looking for volunteers.

Second, we do well to distinguish between the final manifestation of the kingdom and the present anticipations of it. The final coming together of heaven and earth is, of course, God's supreme act of new creation, for which the only real prototype – other than the first creation itself – was the resurrection of Jesus. God alone will sum up all things in Christ, things in heaven and things on earth.[30] He alone will make the 'new heavens and new earth'. We would not only be kidding ourselves, but committing utter folly, to suppose that our own labours could help in that final great work.

But what we can and must do in the present, if we are obedient to the summons of the gospel, if we are faithfully following Jesus, and if we are indwelt by the spirit, is to build *for* the kingdom. Tom ended his book *The Resurrection of the Son of God* with a very deliberate mention of 1 Corinthians 15:58. Paul says there, after his lengthy and somewhat agitated response to those who deny that there will be a future resurrection, 'So, my dear family, be firmly fixed, unshakeable, always full to overflowing with the Lord's work. In the Lord, as you know, the work you're doing will not be worthless.' The back story is that God intends to put everything under Jesus' feet.[31] But precisely because we do not see 'all things' under his feet now, the Church must get busy in the task of preparing the world for Jesus' cosmic lordship. Because we are incorporated into the new-creation life of Jesus' resurrection, we can commit ourselves to kingdom-work, knowing that what we do is neither 'worthless' nor 'in vain'. What is more – and this is crucial – what we do matters because it carries over into the final new creation. We are not called to tinker in the world and then walk away from it, but to curate creation for its consummation. We are not oiling the wheels of a

---

30 See Ephesians 1:10.
31 1 Corinthians 15:24–8; Hebrews 2:7–9; going back of course to Psalm 8:6.

machine that's about to fall over a cliff. We are not restoring a great painting that's shortly going to be thrown on to the fire. We are not planting roses in a garden that's about to be dug up for a building site. We are – strange though it may seem, almost as hard to believe as the resurrection itself – accomplishing something which will become, in due course, part of God's new world.

If that is true, then, every act of love, gratitude and kindness; every work of art or music inspired by the love of God and delight in the beauty of his creation; every minute spent teaching a severely disabled child to read or to walk; every act of care for a dying patient; every deed of comfort and support for refugees; everything done for one's fellow human beings; everything to preserve and beautify the created order; all spirit-led teaching, every deed that spreads the gospel, builds up the Church, embraces and embodies holiness rather than corruption, every prayer for the heart's longings, and the worship that makes the name of Jesus honoured in the world – all of this will find its way, through the resurrecting power of God, into the new creation that God will one day make. That is the logic of the mission of God. God's recreation of his wonderful world, which has begun with the resurrection of Jesus, continues mysteriously as God's people live in the risen Christ and in the power of his spirit. This means that what we do in Christ and by the spirit in the present is not wasted, not abandoned, not discarded. Our holy labours will last long, all the way into God's new world. In fact, they will even be enhanced there.

We have no idea what precisely this will mean in practice. We are putting up a signpost, not offering a photograph of what we will find when we get to where the signpost is pointing. What we do know is that God's new world of justice and joy, of hope for the whole earth, was launched when Jesus came out of the tomb on Easter morning. We know too that Jesus calls his followers to live in him and by the power of his spirit, and so to be new-creation people here and now, bringing signs and symbols of the kingdom to birth on earth as in heaven. The resurrection of Jesus and the gift of the spirit mean that we are called to bring real and effective signs of God's renewed creation to birth even in the midst of the present age.

Not to produce works and signs of renewal within God's creation is ultimately to collude, as evil does and as empires often do, with the forces of chaos and death themselves. But don't focus on the negative. Think of the positive: of the calling, in the present, to share in the surprising hope of God's whole new creation.

The image we should use, in trying to explain this strange but important idea, is that of the stonemason working on part of a great cathedral. The architect has already got the whole plan in mind, and has passed on instructions to the team of masons as to which stones need carving in what way. The foreman distributes these tasks among the team. One will shape stones for a particular tower or turret; another will carve the delicate pattern that breaks up the otherwise forbidding straight lines; another will work on gargoyles or coats of arms; another will be making statues of saints, martyrs, kings or queens. They will be vaguely aware that the others are getting on with their tasks; and they will know, of course, that many other entire departments are busy about quite different tasks as well. When they've finished with their stones and their statues they will hand them over, without necessarily knowing very much about where, in the eventual building, their work will find its home. They may not have seen the complete architect's drawing of the whole building with 'their bit' identified in its proper place. Nor may they live to see the completed building, with their work at last where it belongs. But they will trust the architect so that the work they have done in following instructions will not be wasted. They are not, themselves, building the cathedral; but they are building *for* the cathedral. When the cathedral is complete their work will be enhanced and ennobled, and will mean much more than it could have meant as they were chiselling it and shaping it down in the stonemasons' yard.

The work we do in the present to build *for* the kingdom gains its full significance from the eventual consummation of the kingdom in the time appointed by God. Applied to the mission of the Church, this means that we must erect in the present the signs of that kingdom, providing a preview of what everything will look like when God is 'all in all', when his kingdom has come and his will

is done 'on earth as in heaven'. When the people of the new creation behold its wonder and beauty, it should strike them with an
acute sense of déjà vu, as if to remind them of a prayer they once
heard prayed, an act of mercy they saw performed, a song that they
had once sung that now echoes all around them, a sermon about
Jesus that they now see spring to life, a cry for justice that is now
answered, and a love that was even better than what they were told.
We build for the kingdom, because what we do for the King carries
forward into his royal realm.

Why and how am I to build for this kingdom?

You might be reading this and thinking, 'I'm no pastor or prime minister, neither evangelist nor entrepreneur. I'm happy to watch others
build for the kingdom from the sidelines, and clap when necessary.'
True, not all of us are called into the vocations of ordained ministry
or even full-time kingdom-ventures. Bills must still be paid, young
children or elderly parents must be cared for, and ordinary life does
not grant sabbaticals. But one must be wary of indifference masquer-
ading as humility, as if to say I am too insignificant to make a difference. As if to presume that God cannot use me, though he has used
people less educated and less fortunate than me. Do not fall into the
sin – yes, we should use that word – of becoming merely a religious
consumer rather than a kingdom-contributor.

Whatever your age, ableness, sex, education, limitations, fears,
stage of life or self-doubts, you have something to contribute to the
coming kingdom. Why else is the spirit given, other than to convict
us, inspire us and empower us to do what we would not ordinarily be able to do ourselves? Let your heart be burdened by the needs
you see about you. Let your mind be haunted by a great missionary task that remains unfinished. Let your conscience be pricked
by a grave injustice that goes on blighting your land. Then, as far
as you are able, in your season of life, pick one ministry in your
church to help with and one cause to partner with. In Tom's case,
he has taught Sunday school in churches, administered a cathedral,

overseen a diocese, taught in theological colleges, sought to heal ruptures in the Anglican Communion, and been part of the Jubilee campaign to end the ridiculous and unpayable amount of debt that burdens developing countries. As for Mike, he has led Bible studies for Military Christian Fellowship, been a military chaplain's assistant, led youth groups, had a brief stint as an Anglican curate, advocated for religious freedom and gambling reform, and lectured in theological colleges. That's us building for the kingdom, but what about you? What can you build for in your own home, whether in Oxford, the Ozarks, or in Oklahoma City?

Look around. We live in interesting times, dire times, dangerous times, tragic and terrible times. What will you do with your life? Give it over into staring into a luminous screen or do something that echoes in God's new creation? The world needs kingdom-minded Christians now more than ever. Find some friends to meet with and pray the words of Psalm 31 for the families of Ukraine. Join a group to promote peace between Israelis and Palestinians. Email your local Member of Parliament or Congress and tell them your most pressing concerns. Find out which organisation best assists those recovering from addiction in your town and make a generous donation. Mentor a university student who lives far from family. Ask your pastor how you might pray for him or her and where you could potentially serve given your abilities and interests. Put your faith where your fear is; fill your mind with things of love, not the love of things.

Perhaps the single greatest threat is not the rise of secularism or the emptying of churches, but the apathy and indifference of the churches that are still here. People too self-absorbed and too affluent to care for anything outside their own social media bubble, beyond their own circle of friends, and beyond the view of their front lawns. Too many so-called disciples committed to Jesus to the point of convenience, not to the point where their discipleship costs them anything. Yet Jesus bids us all to come and follow him, to leave worldly trinkets behind and to do hard things, crazy things and impossible things, for no other reason than that he is our king, walking alongside us, suffusing our earthly endeavours with the energy of the spirit.

Will serving in public office build for the kingdom?

A question we must consider is whether the vocation to 'build for the kingdom' can apply to a Christian serving in public office. Of course, this is a way fraught with as much danger as reward. One can achieve much in public office, serving in a local council, a state legislature or a federal senate, or even within a government department. One can do great good for a great many people. But one can also do much damage if bad decisions are made or if political expedience proceeds at the expense of public interest. Plus, there's the temptation to see power as an end in and of itself; a means to influence, status and wealth; or else as an opportunity for corruption and grift. Even if one starts out with the noblest of intentions, those intentions can be worn down by cynicism or ruined by greed. They can end up gaming the system rather than bettering the system. To be a Christian in politics is to be like 'sheep surrounded by wolves'. Therefore, one must be 'as shrewd as snakes, and as innocent as doves'.[32]

All that is true of politics even without bringing God into it. To understand political office as a Christian vocation is obviously prone to manifold abuses. Anyone claiming that God is on their side or that they alone represent the position that God endorses is treading on dangerous ground, perhaps even thin ice, for God is not mocked by such human hubris. It is sheer arrogance to claim that one has a special relationship with God so that our challengers and critics are opposed to God if they are opposing us. One can aspire to have God on one's side in politics, but one must never claim it for certain, nor boast of it as a matter of indubitable fact.

Those warnings aside – the temptations of power and the dangers of mixing God and politics – it can be a great service to one's nation to have men and women of deep Christian conviction in public office. We should not be seeking to lord it over others, but to leaven

---

32 Matthew 10:16.

society with Christian influence.[33] If there is one failing of our liberal democracies, it is that our political systems have encouraged career politicians who have never run a farm or a shop or a school or a ship, and who lurch from utopianism, which gets most of them into politics in the first place, to pragmatic power-seeking, which is what they turn to when Utopia fails to arrive on schedule. When Christian men and women have confidence in their convictions, have experience of life's struggles, see public office as a means, not an end, seek the common good rather than limited privilege, act transparently and respect the rule of law, and cherish consensus rather than stirring up partisan frenzy – then we are seeing people with a real opportunity to build for the kingdom.

Someone might reply to this by asking, 'Shouldn't government be "secular"?' The answer is, 'Yes, it should.' The problem is that secularism is not what most people suppose it is.[34] There are many secularisms and different varieties in the UK, France, Japan, Turkey, China and the USA. Secularism can be anti-religious in ethos and execution, in that it seeks to eradicate the public expression of religion and discourage adherence to a religion. But that is not the only kind of secularism. Secularism in its best and most benign sense is a safeguard, both against a theocracy (in the sense of power-hungry clerics supposing themselves to be the sole and infallible conduits of divine revelation) and against government interference in religion. Secularism is what protects the State against a mad mullah seizing power just as much as against atheist fanatics trying to eradicate religion. Generally, and for the better, Western liberal democracies have normally adopted inclusive models of secularism that do not burden people with the religion of others, while safeguarding religious freedom even for minorities. Such a framework enables

---

33 Mark 10:42; Matthew 13:33. Vincent Bacote, 'A Kuyperian Contribution to Politics', in *Cultural Engagement: A crash course on contemporary issues*, ed. Joshua D. Chatraw and Karen Swallow Prior (Grand Rapids, MI: Zondervan, 2019), p. 237.

34 See Michael F. Bird, *Religious Freedom in a Secular Age: A Christian case for liberty, equality, and secular government* (Grand Rapids, MI: Zondervan, 2022); Luke Bretherton, *Christ and the Common Life: Political theology and the case for democracy* (Grand Rapids, MI: Eerdmans, 2019), pp. 227–57; and Jacques Berlinerblau, *Secularism: The basics* (New York: Routledge, 2022).

widespread political participation, since there should be no religious test or exclusion for serving in public office. In a liberal society with a secular government, governments govern on behalf of people of all faiths and none. Accordingly, their assemblies and parliaments can reflect the demographic diversity in the members elected to parliament, whether Christian, diverse types of Christian or non-Christian.

But that is not to say that religion cannot speak into our political world. Even with a healthy notion of the separation of Church and State, those governed may still appeal to a common consensus and deploy religious resources to urge the State to create a society that benefits people of all faiths and none. At the end of the day, governments make laws, laws are based on policies, policies are based on values, and values are shaped by, among other things, religion. In which case, as long as people of faith can vote, discuss politics, run for public office and serve in government, then religion is always going to have a voice in our political theatres. Such is the 'holy ambivalence', as James Smith calls it, between faith and politics.[35]

To insist that religious considerations can never be brought into the political realm would be impractical (since people cannot compartmentalise their beliefs), impossible (because Church and State relationships are not always clear-cut, as we see for instance in education and the charities sector) and illegal (because you cannot disenfranchise people of faith).[36] In a pluralistic democracy, citizens should feel free to engage in political persuasion based on religious premises.[37] Indeed, democratic and pluralistic societies need to make room for religious voices and religious communities amid the wider sway of voices that can be heard in the public square.[38] The British abolitionist movement of William Wilberforce and the civil rights movement of Martin Luther King were religious rather

---

35 James K. A. Smith, *Awaiting the King: Reforming public theology* (Grand Rapids, MI: Baker, 2017), p. 16.

36 Amos Yong, *In the Days of Caesar: Pentecostalism and political theology* (Grand Rapids, MI: Eerdmans, 2010), p. 84.

37 This is the main argument of Jeffrey Stout, *Democracy and Tradition* (Princeton, NJ: Princeton University Press, 2005), esp. ch. 3.

38 Smith, *Awaiting the King*, p. 135.

than secular political movements. Furthermore, the presence of a Christian voice in Western parliaments should be unsurprising because most Western nations are founded on a Christian heritage. We should therefore expect that Christian values will be reflected, directly or indirectly, in the debate, discourse and legislation that transpire in public.

In a healthy liberal democracy, Christian voices will not be stymied, but neither will non-Christian voices be censored. There should be limits on a Christian influence in government; it must never be absolute. Here we do well to remember that the whole purpose of Christian influence is not the pursuit of Christian hegemony but the giving of faithful Christian witness. Christian hegemony treats Christians as a type of invisible ruling class or an unspoken civil religion that demands public assent. In contrast, Christian witness is offered in a spirit of persuasion, rather than in a spirit of pursuing raw public power. By 'witness', we mean offering a type of 'faithful presence', as James Davison Hunter calls it, in public institutions, where any power wielded is redemptive and relational rather than concerned with power attained by any means.[39] Christian hegemony strives to make Christianity the official religion of the land by playing on fears and prejudice, whereas Christian witness is Christians armed with only persuasion and their own moral authority to win over hearts and minds. One can appeal to a shared Christian heritage, even codify Christian values if it meets with popular consent, but one should never invoke the religion or lack thereof of one's opponents, nor press for modern equivalents of blasphemy laws or heresy trials.

Should we just stick to religion?

In September 1974, Archbishop Michael Ramsey visited Chile under its new right-wing regime. While he preached in church, an armed guard waited outside and asked *The Observer*'s correspondent

---

39 James Davison Hunter, *To Change the World: The irony, tragedy, and possibility of Christianity in the late modern world* (New York: Oxford University Press, 2010).

as he left: 'Was there any politics in it? He must stay with things of the soul, because politics is for us' – the last remark was accompanied by a tap of the gun under his arm.[40] Ramsey was no shrinking violet and not afraid to speak out on political issues, but among the disturbing features of the soldier's remark is the fact that a large number of practising Christians would probably agree with him. The Western world in general has bought heavily into the Enlightenment belief that 'sacred' and 'secular' are divided by an unbridgeable gulf. In that setting, it makes sense to tell Christian people to stop meddling in political matters, stick to spiritual things, stay in your lane of pious niceties and keep your religious sentiments to yourselves. But the compartmentalisation of the spiritual and secular is foreign to Scripture and to most of church history.[41] Secular government is still a divine servant and is therefore theological; the Church's existence cannot be divorced from life within the public sphere and is therefore political.

What looms over this whole discussion is of course the two-realms or two-kingdoms theology which purportedly divides everything between the sacred and the secular, trying (often in a clumsy fashion) to partition the 'spiritual' or 'eternal' domains from the 'secular' or 'temporal'. This division was aptly spelled out at the end of the fifth century by Pope Gelasius I when he wrote to Emperor Anastasius, saying, 'Two there are, august Emperor, by which this world is ruled: the consecrated authority of priests and the royal power.'[42] Eventually, the Byzantine emperor Justinian I would parrot the same thought:

A distinction is drawn between the imperial authority and the priesthood, the former being concerned with human affairs and the latter with things divine; the two are regarded

---

40 Owen Chadwick, *Michael Ramsey: A life* (Oxford: Clarendon Press, 1990), p. 229.

41 On which, see Wright, *History and Eschatology*, ch. 1. Also Smith, *Awaiting the King*, pp. 34–5.

42 Cited in *From Irenaeus to Grotius: A sourcebook in Christian political thought, 100–1625*, ed. Oliver O'Donovan and Joan Lockwood O'Donovan (Grand Rapids, MI: Eerdmans, 1999), p. 179.

as closely interdependent, but, at least in theory, neither is subordinated to the other.[43]

Now this division plays out very differently throughout church history, and what follows is going to be a notoriously terse summary of a few key moments which shows that the distinction is not so cut and dried. The relationship between the sacred and the secular is messy and ambiguous, with kings and popes often trying to get the better of one another. In the fourth century, there was Eusebius of Caesarea and his panegyric to Constantine as the earthly manifestation of the heavenly sovereign who now offers patronage and protection to the Church. Eusebius here places the Church in a subordinate and almost sycophantic relationship to the emperor. But that's not the whole story. In the same century, Ambrose of Milan could rebuke the emperor Theodosius I for the Thessaloniki massacre, while John Chrysostom rebuked the same emperor for interfering in church affairs as well as for avarice and mistreatment of rivals.[44] The bishops of the fourth century did not let the imperial powers have it all their own way.[45]

In the fifth century, Augustine worked out his views on Church and State between, on the one hand, the Donatists who rejected the Church's cosiness with its former persecutors and, on the other hand, the fact that the Roman Empire in his own day was crumbling. This led Augustine to contrast two cities, the city of God with the city of man, cities that intersect and interact. One is

---

43 Cited in *The Oxford Dictionary of the Christian Church*, ed. F. L. Cross and E. A. Livingstone, 3rd edn (New York: Oxford University Press, 1997), p. 916.

44 See Timothy D. Barnes, *Constantine and Eusebius* (Cambridge, MA: Harvard University Press, 2006); and J. H. W. G. Liebeschuetz, *Ambrose and John Chrysostom: Clerics between desert and empire* (Oxford: Oxford University Press, 2011).

45 Eusebius, Ambrose and Chrysostom display a juxtaposition of attitudes towards the Roman Empire. Eusebius regarded the Roman Empire as God's chosen vessel to promote the spread of Christianity (*Oration in Praise of Constantine* 16.4). Ambrose believed that the emperor should promote Christian teachings and values and also be subject to Christian discipline (found abundantly in his *Letters*). Chrysostom tended to emphasise that Christians belong more to heaven than to any earthly city and that the Roman Empire was a necessary stage before the coming of the Antichrist (*Homily 16 on 2 Corinthians* and *Homily 4 on 2 Thessalonians*). The point we are pressing is that the entire Church did not, despite common misconception, prostrate itself before Constantine and his successors and give them carte blanche.

holy, good and true, while the other one is fleshly and seductive. Augustine's city of God never reforms or redeems the city of man. Rather, it resists it in order to outlast it.

Further down the corridors of history we encounter medieval notions of the Church sacralising earthly kings, such as when Pope Leo III crowned Charlemagne as Holy Roman Emperor on Christmas Day in AD 800. But debates later ensued with regard to the Church as a spiritual authority over earthly rulers and the divine right of kings over religious matters in their realms. In the eleventh century, we have an epic confrontation between Pope Gregory VII and Henry IV of Germany about the extent and limits of papal authority. The medieval period was not monolithic: it had moments of the Church resisting the State, supporting the state, trying to usurp the State, or attempting to create a state within the State.

Among Protestants, Luther envisaged the two kingdoms as two divinely appointed instruments for dealing with temporal and spiritual matters, though his views oscillated on how much magistrates should interfere in church matters. Anabaptist theologians advocated the partition of Church and State and stressed the separation of the Church from the realm and reach of the State. The Reformed churches developed the notion of clergy and magistrates as mutually disciplining one another. Such a view might have sounded good, but it became problematic after the Peace of Westphalia in 1648, which led to newly created nation-states in which the principle of religious tolerance made it necessary to loosen the Church–State relationships.

The Enlightenment's project of splitting off what came to be called 'religion' from the rest of life was radically embodied in the First Amendment of the US Constitution, with its strict separation of Church and State. This has been harder to maintain than might originally have been imagined, with some eager to embrace a motto such as 'In God we trust' as a principle of the US republic and others equally eager to challenge it. In neo-Reformed accounts of 'sphere sovereignty', Jesus is lord over each sphere of life through different agents, each of which is accountable to God. In British Radical Orthodoxy, Christianity is not just another 'ism' but more like a metaverse of meaning above politics, with its liturgies providing symbols of resistance against pernicious ideologies and institutions.

If we had time, we could mention too the long tradition of Catholic Social Teaching about government, canvass the interesting relationship between Byzantine rulers and clergy and their attempt to achieve a 'symphony' of Church and State concord, trace the origins of Christian socialism, delve into Liberation Theology, Pentecostal political theology and more. The point is that 'Caesaropapism' and 'inseparable wall between Church and State' have never been the only two options. In every age, every church has had to discern what it meant then and there to say that Jesus has 'all authority' not only 'in heaven' but also 'on earth',[46] working this through in terms of the Church–State relationship, balancing sacred and secular, with the Church discovering what it might mean to be 'in the world' but not 'from the world',[47] to bear theo-political witness without becoming a theocratic menace.

Whatever version of Church–State relationships one prefers or gestures towards, in no circumstance does it require Christians to abandon public witness or to avoid taking political stances. Even Anabaptists and Mennonites who are allergic to civil religion and collaboration with government still find themselves called to civil action and to advocate for things such as pacifism and action on poverty and racial injustice. Yes, there are risks involved in public forays of faith into the public sector, but there are also risks if one does not speak out. Politics is like fire: get too close and you will burn; stay away and you will freeze. One need only consider the work of people such as the British archbishop William Temple or the American theologian Reinhold Niebuhr to see how Christians can shape, for the better, the political settlement of their day. And that is without even considering the positive legacy of Christians in advocating everything from the abolition of slavery, to indigenous rights, to action on poverty and environmental stewardship. Even

---

46 Matthew 28:18.
47 John 17:14–16.

if there are two kingdoms,[48] it does not mean that Christians are prohibited from moving between them or working among them. We are not required to stick to 'spiritual things', even if that means that some political leaders will excoriate us as 'meddlesome priests' or 'God-bothering nuisances'. It is our commitment to Jesus that means that we do sometimes have to make a meddlesome nuisance of ourselves.

What stops us collapsing our kingdom-hope into present projects is the not-yet of Jesus' reign. John of Patmos looked forward to the day when 'the kingdom of the world has passed to our Lord and his Messiah . . . and he will reign forever and ever', a day which seemed far from his own time, beset as it was with the evils wrought by imperial monsters.[49] Or else, the writer to the Hebrews, reflecting on Psalm 8, knew all things would one day be subject to Jesus, but recognised that 'as things are at present, we don't see everything subjected to him'.[50] What we can do at present is 'seek the welfare of the city' in whatever city or village we sojourn, direct institutions such as government towards their God-given tasks of administrating justly as Paul taught, lead wisely like a Joseph when called to serve, give advice to power like Daniel when asked, deliver (as Huldah did) words of prophetic warning and encouragement to rulers, and pray for our political leaders so that we might lead a peaceable life and be known for our godliness. We can colonise earth with the redemptive power, life, beauty and joy of the kingdom to come, yet always with the sober realisation that we'll only ever be an outpost, a signpost, or a billboard of how God intends humans to be his covenant partners in the magnificent display of his sovereignty over the new creation.[51]

---

48 The best recent exponent of 'two kingdoms' political theology is David VanDrunen, *Politics after Christendom: Political theology in a fractured world* (Grand Rapids, MI: Zondervan, 2020). For a discussion of different models of two-kingdoms theology and a critique of these models, see Benjamin B. Saunders and Simon P. Kennedy, 'Characterising the Two Kingdoms and Assessing Their Relevance Today', *Calvin Theological Journal* 53 (2018): 161–73.

49 Revelation 11:15.

50 Hebrews 2:8.

51 Drawing on Jeremiah 29:7; Romans 13:1–5; Genesis 41:37–57; Daniel 2, 4, 5; 2 Kings 22:14–20; Philippians 3:20–1; 1 Timothy 2:1.

When we read the Bible, therefore, we must be aware of the false dichotomies, the foreign categories and the freighted presuppositions that people project upon it. True, the gospel cannot be reduced to a this-worldly project of social betterment. But neither is the gospel an escapist drama for the soul pining for the angelic decor of heaven. If we go that route of spiritual escapism, supposing that the gospel has nothing to do with power, politics, economics and injustice, we are embracing a perspective totally alien to the testimony of the prophets, the teaching of Jesus or the witness of the apostles. If Christians had stuck to 'spiritual' things, then there would be no William Wilberforce, no Martin Luther King, whose lives throbbed with the pursuit of justice precisely as the expression of their deeply cherished faith. There would have been no Velvet revolution in Czechoslovakia and no Christmas revolution in Romania in 1989 if Christians had not taken a stand and acted against Communist authoritarianism.

The case for holistic kingdom-action

The gospel calls us to believe in Jesus Christ, to belong to the Church and to build for the kingdom. If we perform that role properly, we will walk in the way of the cross, and build – right under Caesar's nose! – things that challenge the edifices of totalitarian regimes, that show forth the beauty of God's new creation, that demonstrate that there is a different way to be human, liberated from the lusts of pleasure and power, attaining a genuine human life by conforming to the image of the Son of God. We are to be a 'kingdom of priests'[52] and a 'royal priesthood'[53] in a world savaged by sin, ravaged by death, distraught with despair and destroyed by despots.

Your faith is your defiance against the idols of this world. Your love is your rebellion against the powers of this evil age. Your church is not a retirement village for moralising geriatrics. Your church is supposed to be more like a boot camp for soldiers of Jesus who

---

52 See, with variations of wording, Exodus 19:6; Revelation 1:6; 5:10.
53 1 Peter 2:9.

go out into the world wearing the full armour of God, preaching reconciliation with God, loving their neighbours, sowing good deeds in the soil of hurting hearts, and becoming the scourge of the corrupt and the champion of the weak. We undertake these tasks in such a way as to make clear that Jesus is worthy of our worship. Such things, indeed, are the acts of worship that we lay before his feet.

To do that kind of work, to engage in that kind of holistic mission, will require from time to time doing some public theology. This means that we might be compelled to offer some political commentary, to take a stand in a protest, or to run for public office to effect change. If it is obviously unwise to make politics one's religion, it is no less foolish to think that the life of faith has nothing to do with our political discourse and its legislative chambers.

Within our responsibility to build for the kingdom, there are different levels of interaction between the Church and the official rulers. Romans 13 enunciates the minimal position: being a Christian does not mean being an anarchist. The Creator intends his human creatures to live in social relations, which need order, stability and structure. As we have already said, God made the world in such a way that it would flourish under the delegated authority of humans.

Among these ways will be a full outworking of the implications of Philippians 2:10–11. If it is true that the Church is called to announce to the world that Jesus Christ is Lord, then there will be times when the world will find this distinctly uncomfortable. The powers that be will need reminding of their responsibility, more often perhaps as the Western world moves more and more into its post-Christian phase, where, even when churchgoing remains strong, it is mixed with a variety of idolatries too large to be noticed by those who hold them, and where human rulers are more likely to acknowledge the rule of this or that 'force' than the rule of the Creator. And if the Church attempts this task of reminding, of calling the powers to account for their stewardship, it will face the same charges, and perhaps the same fate, as its Lord. It is at that point that decisions will have to be made, as it will be at that juncture that faithfulness will exact a heavy price from those who refuse to shut up, sit down or walk away. For, if we are found saying that 'we must obey God, not human beings'[54] and seen to be 'turning the world upside down',[55] then the Caesars, Kaisers, tsars, technocrats and plutocrats, who inhabit the privileged heights of culture, corporations and Congress, will make their displeasure known and felt. And there we will most assuredly have the true metal of our faith tested, either to have our complicity purchased with gold, or to bear the cost of irritating a godless civil power by our unwavering allegiance to Jesus and his gospel.

There are many ways of being Christian, of building for the kingdom, and even being political as a Christian. Whatever path one discerns between Church and State, it should be agreed that the separation of the gospel and politics, which is eminently popular in certain shrill branches of contemporary Evangelicalism, will not do. We cannot abandon politics to those who carry guns, or for that matter to those who have access to our metadata. It should also be agreed that a healthy pursuit of the political implications of the gospel will not allow us to use our faith purely in the interest of depositing religious capital into the coffers of political leaders. This implies that the support of a leader by Christians is a transactional exchange, a Christian endorsement of a candidate for the promise of keeping Christianity culturally hegemonic. Yes, sometimes it is clearly a matter of picking the least bad option and a strategic choice of which battles should be fought first. But making Christianity powerful is not the same thing as making the country authentically Christian. Our goal should be promoting the gospel to bring people into the family of faith, not pandering to political leaders so that they might let us share their podium. Christian 'values' – a term open to notorious abuse – should not be reduced to trite slogans. Nor does promising to privilege Christianity compensate for a lack of character or for policies that benefit the rich at the expense of the poor. Let us beware of those who tell Christians to mind their

---

54 Acts 5:29.
55 Acts 17:7.

own business, just as much as we rebuff those who offer Christians power and privilege at the price of their silence or compliance.

We pray for God's kingdom to come on earth as it is in heaven. If all of us are to be true to the giver of the prayer, and to those in the first Christian generation who prayed it and lived it, then we must be building for, and working and praying for, the kingdom. We must act in all earnestness to hold the State accountable and remind it, whether this is believed or not, that even the State is answerable to the Lord Jesus. This lordship is established neither by terror nor by tanks, but by the fruit of the spirit manifesting itself wherever the followers of Jesus may go. Such prayer, and such action, constitute the Church's 'programme'. This theo-political vision shapes all that Jesus' followers must 'do' in his world.

5

The Church between Submission and Subversion

The Church in the shadow of empires

When the news broke in 1945 that the Japanese Empire had surrendered, one national leader responded by quoting the words of Psalm 9:5: 'You have rebuked the nations; you have destroyed the wicked; you have blotted out their name for ever and ever.' The leader who quoted that passage of Scripture was not British prime minister Winston Churchill, nor Free French general Charles de Gaulle, not even the American president Harry S. Truman. It was the Chinese Nationalist leader Chiang Kai-Shek who led a loose coalition of warlords and guerrilla fighters against the Japanese occupation.[1]

Chiang was drawn to this passage for obvious reasons. Psalm 9 celebrates the fact that God's justice triumphs over the wicked, neither ignoring the pleas of the oppressed nor allowing evildoers to prosper. Any nation with ambitions for wickedness fails because:

> YHWH sits enthroned for ever;
> he has established his throne for judgement.
> He judges the world with righteousness;
> he judges the peoples with equity.
> (Psalm 9:7–8)

---

1 Tom Holland, *Dominion: How the Christian revolution remade the world* (New York: Basic, 2019), p. 12, drawing from Rana Mitter, *Forgotten Ally: China's World War II, 1937–1945* (Boston, MA: Houghton, Mifflin & Harcourt, 2013), p. 362.

People of faith, or even just people on the margins, when faced with injustice and inequality, take solace in the fact that God is not an amoral absentee landlord. Rather, God is the God of creation and covenant, who, because of his faithfulness to both, intends to 'put the world to rights'.[2] While Chiang's religious beliefs were somewhat eclectic, incorporating Buddhist and Confucian elements, nonetheless it appears that Christianity was very important to him, helping him to get through several national and personal crises, such as the Xi'an Incident when he was temporarily arrested by his own military subordinates. Christianity, at least the Methodist form that he became involved with, provided a lens through which Chiang understood the volatile years of the Second World War. It was about evil empires being brought down by the just judgement of God.[3]

The question of how the churches should relate to the empires of our own age is genuinely pressing, even urgent. For we live in an age of immense social upheaval and geopolitical uncertainty. Some nations and alliances are declining, while new empires are emerging. It is a time of wars and rumours of wars. We face a looming threat of climate catastrophe and continuous economic turmoil. The world around us is changing, politically, technologically, economically and religiously. In the midst of all these convulsions we must confront the question of how churches are to relate to these emerging empires, technocratic regimes, and democracies beset with internal infighting. We need to think about what the Church's social action and political orientation should be in the highly volatile twenty-first-century environment where the world is being divided between axes of autocracies and loose democratic alliances. The practice of Christian faith requires negotiating different perils and temptations depending on whether one lives in China, Pakistan, Myanmar, Venezuela, Finland or the USA.

---

2   As Tom is fond of saying! See e.g., N. T. Wright, *Simply Christian: Why Christianity makes sense* (London: SPCK, 2006), p. 9.

3   See, on Chiang's relationship with Christianity, Bae Kyounghan, 'Chiang Kai-Shek and Christianity: Religious life reflected from his diary', *Journal of Modern Chinese History* 3 (2009): 1–10.

The purpose of this chapter, then, is to formulate a preliminary report on a theology of politics and power. The way we will do that is by pointing to the tensions between Church and State and mapping the different ways in which Christians have responded to tyrannical state authorities.

How should Christians posture themselves before the State?

In the New Testament, there is an inherent tension in how the Church relates to political authority, a tension that carries over into the earliest centuries of Christianity.

On the one hand, there is a positive relationship between the Church and civic powers when the apostles in Acts 2 are 'standing in favor with all the people'.[4] Luke depicts Roman centurions and tribunes as exemplars of faith, or else he narrates how these military officials treated the apostles with fairness and equality before the law.[5] Paul, while in Ephesus, struck up a positive relationship with the Roman officials administrating Asia Minor, to the point where they warned him about visiting the Ephesian amphitheatre.[6] When in captivity in Caesarea, Paul appealed to Caesar because he expected Caesar to exonerate him from the charges levelled against him.[7] Paul, writing to the Romans, said that government, all government, even the Roman Empire with its idolatries and injustices, is appointed by God to administer justice, and public officials, as God's servants, deserve our obedience.[8] Similarly, Peter instructed believers in Asia Minor to be subordinate and submissive to human institutions, including the emperor and his appointed governors, for such is God's will.[9]

Later, the second-century apologist Justin Martyr would write a treatise to the emperor on behalf of Christians precisely

---

4   Acts 2:47.
5   Luke 7:1–10; Acts 10:21–7.
6   Acts 19:30–1.
7   Acts 25:11–12.
8   Romans 13:1–7.
9   1 Peter 2:13–17.

because he believed it was possible for the emperor to recognise Christians as faithful citizens of the empire.[10] Even Tertullian could argue that Christians can call Caesar 'Lord' in a political sense but not a religious sense. They will not pray *to* him but they will pray *for* him. What is more, because of their wishes for his success and prosperity, he is more their Caesar than the Caesar of some pagans![11] This is why the Anglican divine, Richard Hooker, in his *Laws of Ecclesiastical Polity*, argued that the Church should be subject to the authority and laws of the State in matters that did not directly contradict the Church's essential doctrines. According to Hooker, the State had the authority to regulate the external affairs of the Church, such as the building of churches and even ensuring the proper conduct of public worship.

But on the other hand, there is a negative relationship with state authorities in Christian literature. For a start, Jesus was crucified by a Roman governor at the behest of the Jerusalem high priests.[12] The Latin text of the Apostles' Creed says that Jesus *passus sub Pontio Pilato* ('suffered under Pontius Pilate') but it could just as well say *passus sub imperio Romano* ('suffered under the Roman Empire'). When the Sanhedrin ordered the apostles to stop preaching about Jesus, they declined on the grounds that 'We must obey God, not human beings!'[13] There was something subversive, even world-upending, about the Church's message that 'Jesus Christ . . . is Lord of all' and Jesus is 'king'.[14] Plus, for every benevolent and believing proconsul like Sergius Paulus, there was one like Gallio who turned a blind eye to mob violence by Greeks against Jews; or a Felix who wanted to release Paul from imprisonment but only if Paul paid him a bribe.[15] Furthermore, it was Judaean authorities

---

10 Justin's *First Apology* was addressed to the Roman emperor Antoninus Pius.

11 Tertullian, *Apology* 30–4; cf. Justin, *First Apology* 12; Origen, *Against Celsius* 8.73. This is the compromise position over the empire that the Jews also adopted in their relationship with the emperor.

12 Luke 23; Acts 3:13; 4:27; 13:28.

13 Acts 5:29.

14 Acts 10:36; 17:7.

15 Acts 13:4–13; 18:12–16; 24:26.

who had James the son of Zebedee put to death and later James the brother of Jesus.[16]

Paul and Peter, according to tradition, were both martyred in Rome as part of Nero's persecution of the Roman churches. While the persecution of Christians in antiquity was usually spasmodic and local in the second century, the third century saw brutal and empire-wide reprisals against them for refusing to honour the local deities and participate in the imperial cults.[17] No wonder John of Patmos could describe the Roman Empire as a monster rising out of the sea, filled with blasphemies and brutalities, and salivating with greed. John was praying and hoping for the day when the monster and its worshippers would be destroyed by divine judgement.[18] One can understand why Michael Sattler, author of the Anabaptist *Schleitheim Confession*, called Christians to separate from Babylon and Egypt in every respect, meaning that Christians could not even serve in government because they are citizens of heaven, not of earthly domains.

Here's the tension: when do we appeal to Caesar and submit to governing authorities, and when do we tell Caesar we must obey God rather than human authorities and pray for the government to fall into divine judgement? Can we disobey divinely instituted government? Can that disobedience even go so far as passive and active resistance? To those topics we now turn.

Is it okay to disobey?

Polycarp was bishop of Smyrna (Izmir in modern-day Turkey) in the mid second century. Some time around AD 155/156, he was arrested and brought into a stadium where the proconsul, Statius Quadratus, urged him to swear by the genius of Caesar and to curse Christ. Polycarp was warned that, if he didn't obey, he would be executed, either torn apart by wild beasts or burned alive.

---

16 Acts 12:1–2; Josephus, *Ant.* 20.200.

17 See Wolfram Kinzig, *Christian Persecution in Antiquity*, trans. Markus Bockmuehl (Waco, TX: Baylor University Press, 2021).

18 Revelation 13; 20.

The dilemma was that Polycarp acknowledged that 'we have been taught to pay proper respect to rulers and authorities appointed by God, as long as it does us no harm'.[19] But when faced with coercion in matters of faith, even with threats of violence and execution, Polycarp was determined not to renounce Christ when commanded by a Roman official. He retorted, 'For eighty-six years I have been his servant, and he has done me no wrong. How can I blaspheme my King who saved me?'[20]

Note that Polycarp pointed out that the proconsul, though he was the legitimate agent of a legitimate earthly authority, was demanding that he renounce his master, the Lord Jesus, in the affairs over which Jesus was indeed sovereign.[21] In this predicament, Polycarp chose to disobey the state authority, preferring martyrdom to offering a token act of obedience to a regime that had arrogated to itself the religious devotion of its subjects. Polycarp reasoned in this way because Christians are not obligated to obey state authorities if they do harm or if their hubris attains the heights of thinking that they possess heavenly prerogatives. Polycarp chose to disobey the state authorities by refusing to deny Jesus, making instead the 'good confession', just as Jesus commanded his followers.[22]

While disobedience to the State might seem feasible, for many of us, the gnawing doubt of Romans 13:1–3 remains:

> Every person must be subject to the ruling authorities. There is no authority, you see, except from God, and those that exist have been put in place by God. As a result, anyone who rebels against authority is resisting what God has set up, and those who resist will bring judgement on themselves. For rulers hold no terrors for people who do good, but only for people who do evil.

---

19 *Martyrdom of Polycarp* 10.2 (trans. M. Holmes).

20 *Martyrdom of Polycarp* 9.3 (trans. M. Holmes).

21 Nicholas Wolterstorff, *The Mighty and the Almighty: An essay in political theology* (Cambridge: Cambridge University Press, 2012), p. 15.

22 See Mark 8:38; Matthew 10:32–3; Luke 12:8–9; and 1 Timothy 6:12–13.

How do we disobey the state authorities when Paul told us to obey them because they have been appointed by God to be God's servants? Polycarp is one of the first people to allude to the exception to the principle of submission to state authorities.

The problem with Romans 13:1–5 is not its opacity but its clarity, its plain and unqualified call for submission to governing authorities.[23] Paul's words here are a matter of intense debate as to what occasioned them (the looming rebellion in Judaea?), whether Paul would have changed his mind if he had known about the Neronian persecution which in less than ten short years would ravage the Roman churches and result in his own martyrdom (alternative history), and of course the reception history of this passage in Western civilisation (rulers have been eager to quote this passage to keep their Christian subjects in line, and Christian revolutionaries have been eager to try to find a way round it). In any case, governing authorities are to be obeyed because they are appointed by God to exercise justice and are entitled to both respect and revenue.[24]

Peter similarly stressed that Christians should 'be subject to every human institution, for the sake of the Lord: whether to the emperor as supreme, or to governors as sent by him to punish evildoers and praise those who do good'. Such is 'God's will' and extends even to giving 'honour [to] the emperor'.[25] There is a clear call for submission and paying respect to governing authorities. But, unlike in Romans 13:1–5, the exhortation is qualified somewhat. Government is 'human', not divine. Christians are a 'free people' and 'slaves of God', not slaves of the governing authorities. Christians render 'honor', not worship, to the emperor and his agents. Nothing here would require Christians to make sacrifices to Roman gods, offer a pinch of incense to the emperor's *genius*, or set

---

23 Leander E. Keck, *Romans*, Abingdon New Testament Commentaries (Nashville, TN: Abingdon, 2005), p. 311.

24 See Michael F. Bird, *Romans*, The Story of God Bible Commentary 6 (Grand Rapids, MI: Zondervan, 2016), pp. 441–50; Michael F. Bird, *An Anomalous Jew: Paul among Jews, Greeks, and Romans* (Grand Rapids, MI: Eerdmans, 2016), pp. 245–51; N. T. Wright, 'Romans', in *New Interpreter's Bible*, ed. L. E. Keck (Nashville, TN: Abingdon, 2002), vol. 10, pp. 715–23.

25 1 Peter 2:13–17.

forth an offering to household spirits as slaves might be expected to do.[26] Certainly, the inclination and instinct of believers is to submit and pay respect to governing authorities. By living exemplary lives, Christians provide a service, not only to the emperor, but to God. 'Nevertheless,' comments Thomas Schreiner, 'if governments prescribe what is evil or demand that believers refuse to worship God, then believers as slaves of God must refuse to obey.'[27]

We must remember that the exhortations towards submission and obedience given by Paul and Peter are a general principle, not a rule that should apply to every situation in every place in every age. Government is a divinely appointed institution for the common good. That point was generally agreed upon by Greeks, Romans and Jews. The philosopher Plutarch wrote that 'rulers serve God for the care and preservation of men'.[28] In Proverbs, God declares: 'By me kings reign, and rulers decree what is just; by me rulers rule, and nobles, all who govern rightly.'[29] The Jewish sage Ben Sirach said, 'The government of the earth is in the hand of the Lord, and over it he will raise up the right leader for the time.'[30] The Jewish historian Josephus wrote that 'no ruler attains his office save by the will of God'.[31] In the Gospel of John, when Jesus chose to remain silent before Pilate, Pilate chided him with the chilling threat that 'I have the authority to let you go, and the authority to crucify you'. To which Jesus responded (as we saw in a previous chapter), 'You couldn't have any authority at all over me . . . unless it was given to you from above.' Precisely why this earthly magistrate faced the prospect of divine judgement was because God-given authority carries responsibility.[32] Government is a form of common grace instituted by God so that human rulers are appointed to execute justice, security and

26 Travis B. Williams and David G. Horrell, *1 Peter: A critical and exegetical commentary*, International Critical Commentary, 2 vols (London: T&T Clark, 2023), pp. 728–9.

27 Thomas R. Schreiner, *1 & 2 Peter and Jude*, Christian Standard Commentary (Nashville, TN: Holman, 2020), p. 144.

28 Plutarch, *To an Uneducated Ruler* 3.

29 Proverbs 8:15–16.

30 Sirach 10:4.

31 Josephus, *War* 2.140.

32 John 19:10–11.

welfare for the peoples governed. What is more, governments will be held accountable in this age and the next based on how well they govern.

But what if the government requires Christians to do things contrary to their religion, such as offering a sacrifice to an image of Nebuchadnezzar, or bowing down and worshipping the emperor Domitian? Or if the government tries to compel us to affirm or do something which our consciences will not allow us to do? John Calvin was quite aware of this problem and had much to say about it. Calvin wrote that obedience to state officials 'is never to lead us away from obedience to God . . . if they command anything against him, let it go unesteemed'.[33] Also, 'when princes forbid the services and worship of God, when they command their subjects to pollute themselves with idolatry and want them to consent to and participate in all the abominations that are contrary to the service of God, they are not worthy to be regarded as princes or to have any authority attributed to them.'[34] Calvin was worried about a Catholic prince who might force his subjects to attend the Catholic Mass or enforce certain liturgical rites on Reformed churches. Calvin's point needs to be pondered afresh in the light of the predatory secularisms and pernicious paganisms of our own day. Suffice to say, Calvin rightly grasped that obedience to the State was never total or unqualified.

So, is disobedience to government possible for the Christian? The answer is 'yes', for two reasons. First, no earthly institution, whether monarch or magistrate, possesses absolute authority. The authority of the State is not an inviolable *position* but a *performance* of service, a service rendered to God and exercised for the people. The government's authority is, then, conditional upon its performance to meet God's standards of righteousness and to win the consensus of the people in how they wish to be governed.[35] Second, while government is divinely instituted for the common good, and should be obeyed in principle, not every governor is good. Government

---

33 Calvin, *Institutes* 4.20.32.

34 Calvin, *Lectures on Daniel* 6.22.

35 Wolterstorff, *The Mighty and the Almighty*, pp. 47–52, 116.

should not be obeyed in every instance, especially if it interferes with religious liberty, acts unlawfully, or renders harm to its own people.[36]

We might say that God does indeed bring order through government and wants every aspect of his world to be wisely governed through legitimate authorities. But this carries with it both the temptation to distort the vocation of governing and the culpability for doing so; that is, if rulers abuse their God-given position, then they are answerable to God himself. As for those rulers who engage in cruelty, injustice and avarice, they cannot say that they do so with divine sponsorship by virtue of their office. Their legitimacy is forfeit, for only good government can claim the mantle of a divinely appointed authority. Accordingly, God brings order through government but does not ordain every individual ruler.[37] As such, it can be right for Christians to retort to state authorities, 'We must obey God, not human beings!' and refuse to be 'afraid of the king's orders'.[38]

Disobey to the point of shedding blood?

The question then is whether Christians can move from civil disobedience against unlawful authorities to active resistance to the point of violence against a hostile government. It is one thing to say to a blasphemous king such as Nebuchadnezzar:

> If our God whom we serve is able to deliver us from the furnace of blazing fire and out of your hand, O king, let him deliver us. *But if not*, be it known to you, O king, that we will not serve

---

36 Chrysostom, *Homilies on Romans* 24; John Milton, *Defence of the People of England*, section 3. Martin Hengel (*Christ and Power* [Philadelphia, PA: Fortress, 1977], p. 35) wrote: 'What is demanded is no blind, irrational servitude, but a conscious (and thus vigilant and critical) obedience.'

37 Lee C. Camp, *Scandalous Witness: A little political manifesto for Christians* (Grand Rapids, MI: Eerdmans, 2020), p. 116. The same thought was given by John Chrysostom, *Homilies on Romans* 23.

38 Acts 5:29; Hebrews 11:23.

your gods and we will not worship the golden statue that you
have set up.[39]

But it is another thing to do as the Maccabeans did in their uprising against the Seleucids. It was the Seleucids who, through their
king Antiochus Epiphanes IV, tried to eradicate the Judaean way
of life and turn the Jerusalem Temple into a pagan shrine. The
Maccabean uprising rallied around the Jewish law, fought an in-
surgency campaign against the Seleucids, and had as their motto:
'Pay back the nations in full, and obey the commands of the law.'[40]
So, in the face of injustice or tyranny, do you say, 'God will save us
from you, but if not, I'd sooner suffer than serve you' or do you raise
a flag, a cross or a gun, and cry out, 'Pay the pagans back in their
own coin'?

How far is civil disobedience permitted to go? To engage in
peaceful disobedience when the government tries to boss you about
in religious matters is one thing, but what if the government does
evil or harms its own people or even people in faraway places? On
this topic, Calvin was very reluctant to go down the route of civil
disobedience even in the face of mistreatment:

> If we are cruelly tormented by a savage prince, if we are
> greedily despoiled by one who is avaricious or wanton, if we
> are neglected by a slothful one, if finally we are vexed for piety's
> sake by one who is impious and sacrilegious . . . let us then call
> this thought to mind, that it is not for us to remedy such evils;
> that only this remains, to implore the Lord's help, in whose
> hand are the hearts of kings, and the changing of kingdoms.[41]

Calvin maintained that 'the correction of unbridled despotism is
the Lord's to avenge', so that no recourse is left to God's people 'except to obey and suffer'.[42] Calvin's response is that, in the face of

---

39 Daniel 3:17–18, emphasis ours.
40 1 Maccabees 2:68.
41 Calvin, *Institutes* 4.20.29.
42 Calvin, *Institutes* 4.20.31.

tyranny, the faithful must pray hard and hope for the best. But is this the best we can do when faced with an 'unjust tyranny' which declares to Christians, or to any religious or ethnic group, 'Your existence is illegal'?[43] Must we submit to suffering without recourse to passive or active defence?

Calvin's position reflects the wider Christian tradition which remained strongly opposed to tyrannicide. John of Salisbury pointed out that even tyrants are ministers of God. Accordingly, when a certain bishop encountered Attila the Hun, Attila introduced himself as the 'scourge of God'. The bishop welcomed him as a divinely appointed governor, and the gates of the church were opened to him, even though Attila then martyred the bishop. John claimed that the bishop 'had not the audacity to exclude the scourge of God because he knew that his cherished son had been scourged and that there was no power to scourge him except from the Lord'.[44] Many bishops and theologians noted that even David did not murder King Saul when he had the chance, even though Saul was 'a man of blood'.[45] God also raised up tyrants such as Pharaoh, Nebuchadnezzar, Cyrus, Darius and Caesars to prosecute his purposes. The way to get rid of tyrants was patience and prayer.[46]

Unsurprisingly, many later Protestants, especially the French Huguenots and English Puritans, found Calvin's reluctance to embrace insurrection frustrating and unworkable in the end.[47] Many Protestants decided that obedience only applied to legitimate authority, authority that acted with justice and piety. So it was a duty, as well as a rightful desire, that one should actively and violently resist illegitimate government, that is, a government whose tyranny made it an enemy of both God and the people.

---

43 Tertullian, *Apology* 4.

44 John of Salisbury, *Policraticus* 4.1, cited in *From Irenaeus to Grotius: A sourcebook in Christian political thought, 100–1625*, ed. Oliver O'Donovan and Joan Lockwood O'Donovan (Grand Rapids, MI: Eerdmans, 1999), pp. 282–3.

45 1 Samuel 24:1–7; 2 Samuel 16:8.

46 John of Salisbury, *Policraticus* 8.18–20, cited in *From Irenaeus to Grotius*, ed. O'Donovan and O'Donovan, pp. 294–6.

47 Wolterstorff, *The Mighty and the Almighty*, pp. 74–82.

There was precedent for this view, as Thomas Aquinas had noted that authority could be illegitimate for two reasons: first, if it was attained by violent usurpation; and second, if it was exercised in violent and unlawful ways. Aquinas appealed to Cicero's justification of Brutus for killing Julius Caesar who was a tyrant.[48] Aquinas preferred that a tyrant be removed not by 'private persons' but by a 'public authority' such as a senate or council of nobles, a view that was to be influential.[49] John Wycliffe concluded that if God appointed tyrants then that would mean that the sins of tyranny would be attributed to God, which would be a blasphemous proposition, he claimed. For Wycliffe, tyrants are like those kings spoken of in Hosea 8:4: 'They made kings, but not through me . . .'[50]

Accordingly, after the Reformation, we find works such as the tract *Vindiciae contra Tyrannos* (1579) written by an anonymous French Huguenot author under the pseudonym Stephanus Junius Brutus, which argued that monarchs who violated the natural and inalienable rights of their citizens had forfeited their right to rule, and that the people had the right to resist and remove such a ruler by force if need be. Samuel Rutherford's seventeenth-century tract, *Lex, Rex* (1644), contested the idea that Christians must offer unqualified and absolute fealty to oppressive governments. Rutherford gave a theo-political reading of Romans 13:1–7 that showed that resistance, even violent resistance, to tyrannical rule could be warranted.[51] John Milton wrote his *Defence of the People of England* (1651) to reject the notion of the divine right of kings, to distinguish between kingship and tyranny, to declare that, while laws come from a king, liberty comes from God, and to explain that Paul's remarks about submission to rulers only applies to lawful rulers. Similar arguments about Romans 13:1–7 were presented on the eve

---

48 Thomas Aquinas, *Commentary on the Sentences* 44.2.2, cited in *From Irenaeus to Grotius*, ed. O'Donovan and O'Donovan, pp. 328–30.

49 Thomas Aquinas, *On Kingship* 1.6, cited in *From Irenaeus to Grotius*, ed. O'Donovan and O'Donovan, p. 334.

50 John Wycliffe, *Civil Lordship* 1.1, cited in *From Irenaeus to Grotius*, ed. O'Donovan and O'Donovan, p. 492.

51 See Ryan McAnnally-Linz, 'Resistance and Romans 13 in Samuel Rutherford's *Lex, Rex*', *Scottish Journal of Theology* 66 (2013): 140–58.

of the American revolution where patriotic clergy fused biblical interpretation with Whiggish notions of human liberty and conspiracy theories about the British Crown. In contrast, loyalist clergy urged that the British government was God's duly appointed representative on the earth which deserved reverence, not revolution.[52]

One could refer to two different case studies concerning the argument for and against violent resistance against tyrannical government.

First, in 1920s Mexico, there was the Cristero Rebellion, where Catholic peasants took up arms against the Callas regime which wanted either to suppress Catholicism or else to wipe it out altogether. The Mexican government had forcibly closed churches and schools, banned the wearing of clerical clothing in public, murdered hundreds of priests, exiled thousands of priests, and burned down church buildings. There were peaceful and non-peaceful resistance movements. The Cristeros were armed peasants who attacked federal troops garrisoned in several towns and won several military victories. Eventually the anti-clerical laws and anti-Catholic policies were abolished, softened or not enforced, and a peace was brokered. It is debated how successful the Cristeros were militarily and whether the anti-Catholic measures would have been rolled back even without their uprising.[53]

Second, we could consider the role of Pope John Paul II (1978–2005) in bringing down Communism in Eastern Europe. As the bishop of Krakow, Karol Wojtyla (birth name of John Paul II) was considered a harmless and non-ideological cleric by the Polish Communist Party. But when he became pope in 1978, the Solidarity movement he supported slowly but surely ate away at the Communist dictatorships of Europe, especially in his native Poland. Yes, there were other geopolitical factors at play too, but John Paul II had a leading role in bringing democracy and

---

52 See Gregg L. Frazer, *God against Revolution: The loyalist clergy's case against revolution* (Lawrence, KS: University Press of Kansas, 2018), pp. 45–51; Gary L. Steward, *Justifying Revolution: The American clergy's argument for political resistance, 1750–1776* (Oxford: Oxford University Press, 2021).

53 See David C. Bailey, *¡Viva Cristo Rey! The Cristero Rebellion and the Church–State conflict in Mexico* (Austin, TX: University of Texas Press, 2021).

freedom to the peoples of Eastern Europe. It was a revolution that occurred without tanks or guns. When the pope celebrated Mass in Warsaw one time, while calling for Polish independence from the Soviet Union, declaring that Christ cannot be taken from the people, the crowd responded by singing, 'We want God . . . We want God.' The Soviet Union and Eastern bloc were not defeated by violence, but rather by 'trying every avenue of negotiation, dialogue, and witness to the truth, appealing to the conscience of the adversary and seeking to reawaken in him a sense of shared human dignity'.[54] Thus, there is a case for non-violent resistance demonstrated by John Paul II, as well as Martin Luther King, Gandhi and countless others.

Even to consider the prospect of violence as permissible or divinely sanctioned enters into a morally fraught space. There is a reasonable argument for a just war against a foreign invader, but a justification for anti-government revolutionary violence against one's own civic leaders and against one's fellow citizens is more precarious. To take up arms or to use the might of a mob against one's own people is an ethical minefield. We are told by Jesus not to take 'an eye for an eye' and 'when someone hits you on the right cheek, turn the other one towards him'.[55] Paul also taught, 'Never repay anyone evil for evil,'[56] because to resist evil with evil is to create a never-ending spiral that destroys everything and everyone in its path. One could also argue – that is, purely pragmatically! – that non-violent movements tend to be, more often than not, more successful than violent ones.[57]

The ethics of militant resistance and uncivil disobedience is notoriously complex and disputed.[58] Political theorists such as John Rawls have condoned militant and uncivil resistance to authorities

---

54 *Centesimus Annus* (1991), §23.

55 Matthew 5:38–9.

56 Romans 12:17.

57 See Erica Chenoweth and Maria J. Stephen, *Why Civil Resistance Works: The strategic logic of nonviolent conflict* (New York: Columbia University Press, 2011).

58 See helpful discussion in Jason Brennan, *When All Else Fails: The ethics of resistance to state authorities* (Princeton, NJ: Princeton University Press, 2019).

that do not meet the criterion of being 'nearly just'.[59] The Czech Catholic political philosopher and anti-Communist activist Tomáš Halík writes:

> It is not possible to retreat in the face of violence; it is necessary to protect and defend the innocent . . . One can only turn *one's own cheek*, if there is hope that it will put a stop to evil, but not the cheeks of others. They must be defended.[60]

Similarly, Candice Delmas argues that citizens have a 'duty' to engage in uncivil disobedience that is characterised by 'covertness, evasiveness, violence, and offensiveness'.[61] This disobedience could involve lawful and unlawful expressions of dissent, petitions, strikes, boycotts, riots, whistle-blowing, vigilantism, sabotage and, at the extreme end, revolution.[62] Delmas qualifies that by affirming that non-violent disobedience is preferable, one should seek the least harmful option, and one's actions must take into account other people's rights and the common good.[63]

The dilemma is that Delmas applies this imperative to uncivil action, not just to illegitimate and authoritarian governments, but also to democratic and liberal ones where they act unjustly towards immigrants, minorities or even animals.[64] But that leaves us with a predicament as to which injustices deserve uncivil disobedience. Should one target the homes of judges for being pro-life or pro-abortion? Should activists target houses of worship with gun violence for their support of, or opposition to, gun violence? Should one assault and forcibly remove 'scab' labour? Should victims of gambling addiction smash slot machines in a casino? Should

---

59 John Rawls, *A Theory of Justice* (Cambridge, MA: Harvard University Press, 1971), pp. 367–8.

60 Tomáš Halík and Gerald Turner, *I Want You to Be: On the God of love* (Notre Dame, IN: University of Notre Dame Press, 2019), p. 117.

61 Candice Delmas, *A Duty to Resist: When disobedience should be uncivil* (Oxford: Oxford University Press, 2018), p. 44.

62 Delmas, *A Duty to Resist*, pp. 127–8.

63 Delmas, *A Duty to Resist*, pp. 49, 88.

64 Delmas, *A Duty to Resist*, pp. 135, 175.

taxi-drivers vandalise the cars of Uber drivers who put them out of work? Should vegan activists burn down butcher shops? Uncivil disobedience should only be undertaken for the public good and to uphold civil rights, not for the benefit of niche interest groups, nor to promote a self-interested cause. Furthermore, disobedience must be scaled to the detriment that a government performs against its citizens and non-citizens. Even if no government is ideally just, one should not automatically revert to uncivil actions if the government is, in Rawls's language, 'nearly just'.

It may help if we distinguish unjust laws from unjust government.[65] A government can be, for the most part, just, fair and equitable, but still legislate unjust laws which require our petition, resistance and disobedience. Not every unjust law requires maximal civil disobedience, and an unjust government is better removed from office by democratic process than brought down by a violent mob or a military coup. One needs to have criteria for determining unjust laws, evaluating the performance of a government as a whole, considering the consequences of all options,[66] and responding to injustice with effective yet proportional measures. In some jurisdictions, strident yet peaceful advocacy can achieve better results than short-tempered riots. Christian teaching affirms that obedience and respect for government is the norm even if the government is imperfect or unjust in some matters. Civil disobedience is reserved for unjust laws, and uncivil disobedience should be reserved only for violent authoritarians.

The problem is that some governments are tyrannical to the bone and citizens must develop instruments of resistance depending on the degree of tyranny. Wrestling with such questions, one faces the kind of trilemma that Dietrich Bonhoeffer did in the 1930s. Bonhoeffer was confronted with the question of whether to remain in America to lobby the US government to take a hard line against Nazi Germany, travel to India to study pacifism with Gandhi, or

---

65 Benjamin Saunders, *The Crisis of Civil Law: What the Bible teaches about law and what it means today* (Bellingham, WA: Lexham, 2024), pp. 149–50.

66 David VanDrunen (*Politics after Christendom: Political theology in a fractured world* [Grand Rapids, MI: Zondervan, 2020], p. 356) wisely notes: 'Overthrowing Batista may give you Castro. Overthrowing the Shah may give you Khomeini. A revolution itself can produce massive suffering that outweighs the injustice it was meant to remedy.'

return to Germany, join the Confessing Church, and (eventually) take part in the plot to assassinate Adolf Hitler. Would anyone claim there was an easy answer?

The truth is that Christians have been able to survive and even thrive under all sorts of governments, including monarchies, oligarchies, dictatorships, sultanates, liberal democracies, tribal confederations and more, without resorting to violent resistance. We do not think that the regulation of the price of tea and the ambitions of landholding gentry in the American colonies justified the American revolution against British authority. The reading of Romans 13:1–5 used to justify the American war of independence by the colonies was also used to justify the insurrection of the confederacy against the US federal government and its emancipation of slaves.[67] We would want to claim that any uncivil resistance needs to be proportionate and have a criterion for distinguishing between lawful/legitimate and unlawful/illegitimate state authorities. Furthermore, the risk remains that to resist violence with violence creates a never-ending spiral which becomes more oppressive than whatever regime one is staring down. Civil disobedience need not be violent, only subversive, that is, aiming to deter, disrupt or destroy the capacity of a civil authority to maintain or extend its exercise of unjust power.[68]

But then again, we have never felt the lash of a totalitarian government upon our back, had our family members taken away in the night by secret police, found ourselves detained for criticising government policies, had our political opinions censored, seen our churches burned down in front of us, been sent into exile, or witnessed opposition leaders being executed because of their popularity with the masses. Such things could conceivably convince us that there is a case for a just war against an unjust totalitarian regime in one's own nation. Accordingly, perhaps uncivil and/or

---

67 On the political use of the Bible in the American revolution and civil war, see Kaitlyn Schiess, *The Ballot and the Bible: How Scripture has been used and abused in American politics and where we go from here* (Grand Rapids, MI: Brazos, 2023), pp. 21–52.

68 Joseph Pierce and Olivia R. Williams, 'Against Power? Distinguishing between Acquisitive Resistance and Subversion', *Geografiska Annaler: Series B, Human Geography* 98 (2016): 171–88.

militant resistance might be permissible when dealing with a megalomaniac such as Nero, while living under Nazis in Nuremberg, when dealing with a Hindu extremist government in Nagpur, or when Islamic terrorists take over an Iraqi town such as Najaf. As Kenyan Anglican archbishop David Gitari put it, 'Taking arms to fight autocratic regimes should only be done when all other means of bringing the desired political change have failed.'[69] These words carry particular gravity if you know about British savagery in Kenya during the Mau Mau uprising in the 1950s.[70] But most of the time, violence and revolution are not the answer. We must allow peaceful non-violence to be the norm in our opposition to tyranny and injustice.

Of course, that leaves a question hanging in the air: whom are we to resist?

---

69 David Gitari, 'You Are in the World but Not of It', in *Christian Political Witness*, ed. George Kalantzis and Gregory W. Lee (Downers Grove, IL: InterVarsity Press, 2014), p. 217.

70 See Caroline Elkins, *Imperial Reckoning: The untold story of Britain's gulag in Kenya* (New York: Henry Holt, 2005).

6

The Church Resisting the Powers of Today

Whom should we resist?

To recap, we've seen that Christians have a complex relationship with the State, existing between the poles of seeking political favour with civic leaders and being a political nuisance in Jesus' name. Furthermore, while government is instituted by God for public justice, security and welfare, we have concluded that it is permissible to disobey unjust laws and to resist unjust government. That should be done preferably by peaceful means, but with a door slightly ajar to just war against tyrannical government in the most extreme of occasions. Now we wish to explore the type of unjust governments that Christians may find themselves called to resist. This too is not straightforward: it is contested and a moral minefield if ever there was one. What follows is not an exhaustive exploration; it is a selective case study, intended to be relevant to current events in the 2020s.

Against totalitarianism

Totalitarianism comes in many packages, whether Fascist, Communist or theocratic. At the moment, it is fair to say that Fascism exhibits particular notoriety, largely in the light of the haunting story of Germany and the rise of the Nazis. The problem is that Fascism is a specific sociopolitical phenomenon from the first half of the twentieth century that arose under special conditions created by the First World War and the Great Depression. The derogatory label 'Fascist' is now so over-used and over-applied as to be practically meaningless. Today, 'Fascist' is more or less synonymous with 'bad people'. The 'Fascist' label has been used to designate everyone from Brexit voters, to Polish Catholics, to populist political leaders, to gender-critical lesbians, to critics of the Venezuelan government. One wonders if the term needs to be retired.

Nonetheless, we should take heed of Fascist-like regimes who weaponise grievances, valorise militarism, play on ethnic prejudices, and believe that all the nation's problems can be solved by a demagogue carrying a big stick.[1] Such regimes can be found in the Middle East, Africa, Asia, Europe and South America, sometimes supported by the West due to their anti-Communist stance, or their favourable disposition to Western business interests.

Perhaps the hardest thing to grasp is how seductive Fascism was for people. We like to imagine that, if *we* had lived in Germany in the 1930s, *we* would not have followed the masses in either enthusiasm for or complicity with the Nazi regime. But would we have been so allergic to it or actively opposed to it? Nazism was seductive precisely because it promised an immediate fix to parliamentary gridlock, an end to economic chaos, and a refusal to bow to the crushing indemnities and humiliating conditions imposed upon Germany by the Western powers after the First World War. Nazism was not an alien political doctrine that appeared out of nowhere. Nazism succeeded because it embodied what people either believed or wanted to believe.[2] Nazism was an incredibly eclectic world view, combining Darwinian science and pseudo-sciences such as eugenics, and incorporating some aspects of Lutheranism, elements of the

---

1 The word 'Fascism' comes from the Latin word *fascis*, meaning a bundle of rods, including an axe, symbolising the power of a magistrate, stemming from Etruscan civilisation. It was inherited by ancient Rome and then taken up by the National Fascist Party in Italy with Mussolini. Fascism is perhaps best defined as a form of far-right authoritarian ultra-nationalism characterised by dictatorial power and forcible suppression of any opposition, with a strict regimentation of society and government regulation of the economy.

2 Jacques Ellul, *Jesus and Marx: From gospel to ideology* (Grand Rapids, MI: Eerdmans, 1988), p. 4.

philosophy of Nietzsche, the music of Wagner, Nordic mythology, anti-Jewish conspiracy theories, numerology, idealised masculinity, nationalism, militarism, anti-Communism and belief in the magical power of ancient artefacts – it had something for everyone! Nazism appeared to be scientific, spiritual, progressive and effective, the new type of civilisation the world needed. In addition, as a philosophy, Nazism was internally consistent to the point where it appeared self-evident to many people, which is precisely why it attracted supporters from all over Europe.[3]

It is worth noting, too, that Fascism and Communism, for all their differences, both hinge on absolute power put into the hands of the State and its supreme leader. Indeed, Timothy Snyder has argued that the Fascism and Communism that ravaged Eastern Europe should be understood as part of the one phenomenon of authoritarian dictatorship.[4] Tomáš Halík opines that Communist evils tend to be glossed over due to our haunting and horrified fixation on the evils of Fascism:

There has been considerable theological reflection on Nazism and the holocaust, also on Latin America and its quest for liberation, as well as upon the evils of western empires, but considerably little theological attention has been given to the confrontation with communism as an anti-human and authoritarian nightmare.[5]

The Communist leaders Stalin and Mao killed far more people than Hitler, King Leopold of Belgium in the Congo, and the military junta of Argentina put together. Yet Hitler and Fascism remain lodged in Western imagination as the definitive symbol of human evil.

Concerning Communism, it cannot escape our notice that Christianity and Marxism have remarkably similar meta-narratives.

---

3   Peter J. Hass, *Morality after Auschwitz: The radical challenge of the Nazi ethic* (Minneapolis, MN: Fortress, 1988), pp. 13–14, 99.

4   Timothy Snyder, *Bloodlands: Europe between Hitler and Stalin* (London: Basic, 2022).

5   Tomáš Halík, *Patience with God: The story of Zacchaeus continuing in us* (New York: Doubleday, 2009), p. 60.

The Christian story of creation, Fall, sin, Redeemer, redemption, Parousia and consummation finds its parallel in the Marxist story of primitive society, the invention of capital, worker exploitation, the proletariat, the proletarian revolution and Communist utopian society.[6] In addition, there are obvious points of contact between Christian social concerns and Marxist ideology. The Marxist mantra, 'From each according to his ability, to each according to his needs', was not really a deduction about the inevitable forces of history propelling themselves towards a utopia of workers and farmers as much it was a materialistic and industrial appropriation of the Christian concern for the poor, the Christian virtue of justice, and the notion of earth and city as a common treasury for everyone. The Hebrew Bible, the teaching of Jesus, the ethics of the apostles, and the social vision of the church fathers are saturated with concerns about the poor, oppression, injustice and God's radical reordering of power in the hereafter. In the earliest days of the Jerusalem church, the believers held all their possessions 'in common',[7] and the Apostle Paul requested that the Corinthians share from their abundance with the Jerusalem church in a time of famine in order 'that there should be equality'.[8]

Indeed, Basil the Great's *On Social Justice* is an indictment of the injustices of his own day, and Gregory of Nyssa's famous sermon[9] innovatively claimed that slavery violates the laws of God and nature. Both theologians show just how much of abolitionist, socialist, liberationist and Marxist doctrines carry Christian genes. One could even argue that the need for social revolution is championed by none other than the mother of God as Mary's Magnificat celebrates the inversion of power that God's kingdom brings: 'Down from their thrones he hurled the rulers, up from the earth he raised

---

6 Ellul, *Jesus and Marx*, p. 42.

7 Acts 2:44–5; 4:32.

8 2 Corinthians 8:13–14.

9 Gregory of Nyssa, *Hom. Eccl.* 4. See *Gregory of Nyssa: Homilies on Ecclesiastes: An English version with supporting studies*, ed. S. G. Hall (Berlin: De Gruyter, 1993), pp. 72–4.

the humble. The hungry he filled with the fat of the land, but the rich he sent off with nothing to eat.'[10] Marx then was basically articulating a Jewish vision of messianic justice but without God.

The followers of the Messiah can sound obliquely Marxist as they share concerns about evil – whether intrinsic or industrial, cosmic or corporate evils – that leave the poor, vulnerable and oppressed exposed to needless sufferings and manifold injustices. This explains why there arose a tradition of Christian socialism, from the English 'Diggers' of the seventeenth century, to Christian Democratic Socialists of the nineteenth, all the way through to the Catholic Liberation Theologians of the twentieth century.[11] As such, Marx, though a professed materialist and atheist, was 'oddly prone to seeing the world as the Church Fathers had once done: as a battleground between cosmic forces of good and evil'.[12] Indeed, the deist and atheist protests against organised religion from the seventeenth to the twenty-first centuries show evidence of Christian DNA when set in contrast to the vision and values of the ancient world.

Even so, we should note that the similarities between Christian social teachings and Marxism have obvious limits. While there are varieties of Marxism, Marxist regimes always fail in their objectives to lift the poor out of poverty. Marxists end up oppressing their own people with guns and gulags. In addition, for all their cry for equality, some people always end up being more equal than others. George Orwell's critiques of Communism in *Animal Farm* and *1984* contain salient lessons that we should never forget. Above all, Communism is tethered to tyranny. Many of us have friends who have lived under Communist regimes and you will be hard pressed to find one who speaks of such regimes with warmth, fondness and affection. They regard them ordinarily with dread, loathing and trauma.

---

10 Luke 1:52–3.

11 Brazilian Catholic archbishop Hélder Pessoa Câmara famously said, 'When I give food to the poor they call me a saint. When I ask why the poor have no food, they call me a Communist.'

12 Tom Holland, *Dominion: How the Christian revolution remade the world* (New York: Basic, 2019), p. 457.

The ironic thing about Communism is that it is simultaneously too Christian and not Christian enough.

On the one hand, Communism is too Christian in that it constitutes an over-realised Christian eschatology, trying to bring heavenly justice to earth by violent revolution, attempting to manufacture the conditions where 'the last will be first, and the first will be last'.[13] Such a Communist utopia can only be created, Marx said, 'by despotic inroads',[14] so that the road to paradise runs through several caverns of hell. We cannot forget that 'the Kharkov famine [of the Soviet Union] and the Killing Fields [of Cambodia] were perpetrated by atheists in an attempt to realise the most lofty ideals of human perfection'.[15]

On the other hand, Communism is not Christian enough because it lacks a doctrine of total depravity. In Marxism, evil is what capitalists do, what the bourgeois do, what the factory owners do, but it cannot accept that evil lives in the hearts of Communists too. Marxist leaders believe that they 'are exempt from error and can therefore arrogate to themselves the exercise of absolute power'.[16] That is precisely why Aleksandr Solzhenitsyn wrote in his *Gulag Archipelago* that 'the line separating good and evil passes not through states, nor between classes, nor between political parties either – but right through every human heart – and through all human hearts'.[17]

One must therefore remain vigilant against any would-be Christian leaders who attempt to justify authoritarian regimes, who cooperate with them, or who try to reinterpret Christianity to fit with authoritarian dogmas. There are some notorious examples. First, the German biblical scholar Walter Grundmann was a card-carrying Nazi and leading member of the German Christians

---

13 Matthew 20:16 (NIV).

14 Manifesto of the Communist Party, February 1848, ch. 2: https://www.marxists.org/archive/marx/works/1848/communist-manifesto/ (accessed 28 September 2023).

15 Charles Taylor, *Sources of the Self: The making of modern identity* (Cambridge, MA: Harvard University Press, 1989), p. 519.

16 *Centesimus Annus* (1991), §44.

17 Aleksandr Solzhenitsyn, *The Gulag Archipelago* (New York: Harper & Row, 1975), vol. 2, pp. 615–16.

(*Deutsche Christen*). He wrote a book called *Jesus der Galiläer und das Judentum* (*Jesus the Galilean and the Jews*) where he argued that Jesus was from Galilee, and Galilee was known as 'Galilee of the Gentiles'.[18] Therefore, Grundmann concluded, Jesus was not a Jew, but an anti-Jewish Aryan whose Gentile identity had been concealed by Jewish Christians who falsified the Gospels. As if that were not bad enough, in post-war Germany, Grundmann ended up becoming an informant for the East German Stasi and spied on theologians in East and West Germany. Second, Chinese theologian C. S. Song argued that Chairman Mao's Cultural Revolution was a movement of the holy spirit.[19] Song was not only critical of Western colonialism and Western-centric ways of thinking, but also postulated that God was immanently working through Asian cultures, even through Communism, to bring about the kingdom of God in Asia. In doing so, Song gave religious legitimacy to one of the most violent and barbarous repressions in human history. One cannot deny that Western colonial powers oppressed people in northern and southern Asia, but Communist regimes and military juntas have terrorised their own populace far more than any European administration ever did.[20]

We should take heed then of the examples of Christian leaders who have stood up to military and Marxist dictatorships. One naturally thinks of German leaders in the Confessing Church such as Martin Niemöller and Dietrich Bonhoeffer. There was Bishop Oscar Romero in El Salvador, who was assassinated by a right-wing death squad while celebrating Mass in 1980. There is something to be said for reading classic books such as Richard Wurmbrand's *Tortured for Christ* which voiced the plight of Christians in Eastern Europe under Communist regimes.[21] More recently, one should

---

18 Drawing from Matthew 4:15.

19 C. S. Song, 'New China and Salvation History: A methodological inquiry', in *South-East Asia Journal of Theology* 15 (1974): 52–67; see critique in Simon Chan, *Grassroots Asian Theology: Thinking the faith from the ground up* (Downers Grove, IL: InterVarsity Press, 2014), pp. 21–2.

20 So too Ellul, *Jesus and Marx*, p. 58.

21 See also Matthew Heise, *The Gates of Hell: An untold story of faith perseverance in the early Soviet Union* (Bellingham, WA: Lexham, 2022).

consult the writings of Chinese pastor Wang Yi who has forged his own theology of Church and State in the crucible of state persecution. In fact, Yi once said to a police interrogator:

> I am telling you about a power that will last forever. But this power does not demand lands, swords, or all the authority in this day. On the contrary, it is willing to humble itself and submit to the swords and authorities on earth. If you want to use earthly power today to oppress the eternal power, this Scripture has already revealed the end result. History is Christ written large, not Xi Jinping written large.[22]

Let us remember, commemorate, and learn from the courage of men and women, from all Christian traditions, who have had the courage to profess faith and stand for religious freedom in the face of tyranny.[23]

Against Christian nationalism

Christian nationalism is a danger to Christians and non-Christians alike. Now, of course, this depends on what you mean by 'Christian nationalism'. We have no problem with the notion that Christianity has been part of the heritage of this or that nation. Christianity has shaped our constitutions and cultures for the better, and State and Church can cooperate for the common good in providing education, healthcare and pastoral care. One can tussle a bit as to whether there should be an officially established church such as the Church of England. We hasten to point out that even with a state-sanctioned church in the UK, there is still a healthy degree of secularity, religious pluralism and multiculturalism. When we warn of the evils of Christian nationalism, we are warning of the

---

22 Wang Yi, *Faithful Disobedience: Writings on Church and State from a Chinese house church movement*, ed. Hannah Nation and J. D. Tseng (Downers Grove, IL: InterVarsity Press, 2022), p. 184.

23 Also recommended is Timothy Snyder, *On Tyranny: Twenty lessons from the twentieth century* (London: Crown, 2017).

danger of the government trying to enforce Christian hegemony combined with civil religion (that is, an outward and merely cultural version of Christianity). In other words, the danger is that Christians are given special privileges by the State and Christianity becomes an outward display of patriotic devotion rather than part of true religious affection.

The idea that the Christian world needs an anointed Christian leader, a Christian emperor presiding over a Christian empire, is one that has existed since Constantine, and even persists into the present. In fact, quite recently, one prominent British theologian has tweeted, in response to Queen Elizabeth II's passing, that 'the Queen was effectively the Queen of the world . . . perhaps [the] necessary role of Christian world emperor has now fallen on the British monarchy'.[24]

We are all for commemorating Queen Elizabeth II, but we remain unsure if we should valorise her or her successor King Charles III as a 'Christian world emperor'. The danger is that one is approaching the sycophantic position of Eusebius of Caesarea who claimed that the emperor Constantine was hailed by angels and armies alike as 'master, lord, and king'.[25] This christianisation of kingship is not far from those who claimed that US president Donald Trump was a 'new Cyrus'. Many admirers pushed the idea that Trump, despite his bawdy and tawdry behaviour, was a man whom God had anointed to make the USA great again just as God called the Persian king Cyrus to liberate the Judaean exiles in Babylon.[26]

We would naturally be happy to live under the administration of a wise and benevolent Christian leader. Of course, we are also happy to live under a Pharaoh who puts a clever and capable Joseph in charge, or vote for a Nebuchadnezzar who heeds the counsel of

---

24 John Milbank, Twitter, 9 September 2022: https://twitter.com/johnmilbank3/status/1568177131967991808 (accessed 11 September 2023).

25 Eusebius, *Speech for Thirtieth Anniversary of Constantine's Accession* 1, cited in *From Irenaeus to Grotius: A sourcebook in Christian political thought, 100–1625*, ed. Oliver O'Donovan and Joan Lockwood O'Donovan (Grand Rapids, MI: Eerdmans, 1999), p. 60.

26 Isaiah 45:1–13.

a wise man such as Daniel. Even Martin Luther said he'd rather be ruled by a wise Turk than a foolish Christian. Be that as it may, to contend that one needs a king or president, not only to protect institutions such as the Church, but actively to impose the Church's worship on others, is always going to prove ruinous to civil and religious liberties. Such a position would imply that God not only uses governments for justice and judgement, but also needs them as the political sword by which people, whether Christian or not, will be compelled to conform their lives to Christian standards. That is dangerous because to identify any leader as 'YHWH's anointed'[27] or a new 'Cyrus'[28] is to invest a perilous amount of religious capital in a single person. Such a person may prove to be all too human, all too given to corruption, full of depravity and easily seduced by the lust for power. After September 11, 2001, Tony Blair spoke about 'evil' being at large in the world and of his determination to deal with it – almost as though this was a new and unexpected problem – but that with his policies and leadership evil could be conquered. We know where that led.

When such leaders are venerated with religious adulation, the result inevitably is that any critique of them, no matter how valid, is treated as either treason or blasphemy. The UK Parliament, no less than the US Senate, eagerly backed the dangerous and irrelevant call for a war against Iraq. The messianising of leaders to prop up an imagined 'Christian empire' can have dire consequences for social freedoms as well as proving injurious to the integrity of the Church's own witness when it allies itself too closely with an earthly power. Remember that the Scriptures have a special title for someone who claims to possess kingly and religious authority, who is both presidential and priestly: the word is 'Antichrist'. Such a person is against Christ by assuming Christ's own role, because Christ alone is both messianic King and the Great High Priest.[29]

---

27 Cf. Psalm 2:2.

28 Isaiah 45:1.

29 See especially Oliver O'Donovan, *The Desire of the Nations: Rediscovering the roots of political theology* (Cambridge: Cambridge University Press, 1996), pp. 203, 214–15.

Christian nationalism of the kind we have described is bad on every level imaginable. Christian nationalism does not lend itself to a tolerant society since it diminishes the rights of the people of other religions or no religion. It leads to a superficial Christianity rather than to sincere faith and deep discipleship. Political leaders end up pretending to be religious merely to win the favour of their constituents. Christianity is used to justify unchristian policies and actions related to wars, immigration, income inequality, healthcare and a myriad other issues. Remember that even the devil can quote Scripture and try to rub it in the face of Jesus.

The other problem with Christian nationalism is which type of Christianity should be supreme. It is baffling that, in the USA, many Baptists are coming out as supporters of Christian nationalism. It is baffling to us because Baptists fled the religious sectarianism of the British Isles to go to America in the seventeenth century. The reason they fled was because Baptists, and other Nonconformists, were persecuted, discriminated against and cajoled in matters of religious conviction. They went to America so that they could practise their faith without government interference. As we all know, there are different Christian denominations, so which one should be supreme in a Christian nationalist state? Should it be Anglicans, who could then force everyone to baptise their babies, worship using only the Book of Common Prayer, demand adherence to the Thirty-Nine Articles of Religion, sing hymns that equate the British Empire with 'Jerusalem' on earth, and petition heaven with 'God Save the King'? But the same is true whether you put Methodists, Presbyterians or Pentecostals in charge. They could impose *their version* of Christianity upon everyone else or grant special privileges to their version of Christianity. Religious liberty thus protects Christians from other Christians. And, if you are going to give religious liberty to Christians, then why not to non-Christian religions as well? The logical implication of religious freedom for Christians is religious freedom for all people, irrespective of their religion or lack thereof.

Another deficiency of Christian nationalism is that it leads government to try to regulate religion. In Christendom, it was considered normal that the king would defend Christian doctrine and safeguard

Christian moral instructions. This is why Isidore of Seville in around AD 600 claimed that 'secular powers are subjected to the discipline of religion' while secular princes 'may use that power to reinforce church discipline'.[30] In the twelfth century, Thomas Aquinas said:

> The king's duty is therefore to secure the good life for the community in such a way as to ensure that it is led to the blessedness of heaven, that is by commanding those things which conduce to the blessedness of heaven and forbidding, as far as it is possible to do so, those which are contrary.[31]

Calvin similarly thought that monarchs and magistrates should promote and protect religion and morals, so that a regent's role was 'to cherish and protect the outward worship of God, to defend sound doctrine of piety and the position of the church'.[32]

The problem is that, if you take the route of the government as the guarantor of Christian religion, then that requires government to adjudicate in matters of religion, to solve theological disputes and to hold heresy trials. Will the government arrest heretics, license preachers, regulate seminaries and impose Sabbath observance? Martin Luther, at least in his early years, knew that 'heresy is a spiritual matter which you cannot hack to pieces with iron, consume with fire, or drown in water'.[33] Or, as the British philosopher John Locke put it, 'What power can be given to the magistrate for

---

30 Isidore of Seville, *Sentences* 3.51, cited in *From Irenaeus to Grotius*, ed. O'Donovan and O'Donovan, p. 208.

31 *St Thomas Aquinas: Political writings*, trans. and ed. R. W. Dyson (Cambridge: Cambridge University Press, 2002), p. 53.

32 Calvin, *Institutes* 4.20.2; followed by Turretin, *Institutes of Elenctic Theology* 3.316–36. The *Westminster Confession of Faith* 23.3 (1647) declared that the magistrate 'hath authority, and it is his duty, to take order, that unity and peace be preserved in the Church, that the truth of God be kept pure and entire; that all blasphemies and heresies be suppressed; all corruptions and abuses in worship and discipline prevented or reformed; and all the ordinances of God duly settled, administered, and observed' with 'power to call synods, to be present at them'. Many Presbyterian churches around the world have modified this line so it doesn't grant such authority to the civil powers over their synods. Interestingly, the 1689 *London Baptist Confession*, which uses the *Westminster Confession of Faith* as a template, conspicuously avoids granting the magistrate such authority over Baptist churches.

33 Martin Luther, *Temporal Authority* 502–3.

the suppression of an idolatrous Church, which may not in time and place be made use of to the ruin of an orthodox one?'[34] In a diverse and pluralistic society, governments would be wise neither to privilege one religion, nor to punish people over their religion. Religion is at its most free when government does not interfere with religion or try to adjudicate in matters of religion. Thus, a certain degree of secularity – by which we mean preventing theocracy, enabling the free exercise of religion, and permitting liberty of conscience in religion – is far better than Christian nationalism.

Christian nationalism, in its Protestant form, can lead to a certain degree of Erastianism,[35] where Protestant governments attempted to regulate religion to keep it pure and publicly acceptable. Or else, Christian nationalism, in its Catholic expression, tends to a hierocratic Integralism[36] built on the state-sanctioned purification of religious life and the subjection of secular government to papal authority. These should be differentiated from 'establishment churches' where, due to a mixture of history and heritage, certain states have established churches that have been part of the fabric of society and woven into the social landscape since late antiquity. One thinks here of the Church of England or the Church of Sweden. Contrary to reputation, these churches are not 'Constantinian' or 'theocratic' institutions, but simply attest that, historically, many churches have had a close and cooperative

---

34 John Locke, *A Letter Concerning Toleration* (London, 1689), p. 34.

35 Erastianism is a political doctrine that advocates the supremacy of the State over the Church even in religious matters. It originated in the sixteenth century and was named after Thomas Erastus, a Swiss theologian who supported the subordination of the Church to the State.

36 There is a species of Catholic political thought known as 'Integralism', which postulates the theory that the ideal state is one that is guided by Catholic principles and that the Church should have a direct role in the governance of society. Catholic Integralism is premised on recovering the integration of Church and State (or pope and king) that disappeared after the decline of Christendom and the rise of nation states in the eighteenth and nineteenth centuries. There is a tension in Catholic thought, exemplified by the differences between the Vatican II document *Dignitas Humanae* (1965) which affirms religious freedom, and the way popes of the late nineteenth and early twentieth centuries had conceived of 'Christ as King' even over civil affairs, such as in Pope Pius XI's encyclical *Quas Primas* (1925). For a critique of Catholic Integralism, see Kevin Vallier, *All the Kingdoms of the World: On radical religious alternatives to liberalism* (New York: Oxford University Press, 2023).

relationship with the government and continue to do so even up to the present. Yes, there is a certain danger of civil religion or cultural Christianity when churches have an established status, but that is simply the price paid for the success of the Christian mission in those countries. Our point is that, whether one exists in a country with a wall of separation between Church and State, or whether there are established churches, the regulation of religion by the State and the punishment of religious dissenters by the State are not conducive to the freedom of worship of a country's citizens. Moreover, using religion to manufacture social and ethnic homogeneity is doomed to give sanction to prejudice and to weaponise religion in the hands of wicked actors.

Christian nationalism also lends itself to feelings of ethnic superiority and promotes interracial tensions especially when Christianity is aligned with 'whiteness'. In countries where one religion is dominant, it is usually dominant among one ethnic group. Thus, religious privileges get fused with the hegemony of one ethnic group and its political apparatuses. For example, in Malaysia, the country is dominated by its Muslim Malay population. Thailand is dominated by its Tai majority who are also majority Buddhist. But Christianity is not an ethnic religion. Christianity is a global religion, not the religious expression of an ethnic identity. As Wolterstorff argues, the Church included Romans but not all Romans. So the Church is not Roman. The Church included Slavs but not all Slavs. So the Church is not Slavonic. Similarly, the Church includes Americans, but not all Americans, so the Church is not American. The Church includes Brits, but not all Brits, so the Church is not British.[37] The Church breaks down the classes, caste systems and ethnic divisions so that God's people are those from every tribe, tongue, ethnic group and nation. Christian nationalism, requiring state interference in religion and ethnic homogeneity, is a threat to the multi-ethnic nature of the global Church.

Finally, we must remember that Christian nationalism is not merely a US phenomenon. There are versions of Christian nationalism is Europe, Africa, Asia, South America and even Australia. Today, the

---

37 Nicholas Wolterstorff, *The Mighty and the Almighty: An essay in political theology* (Cambridge: Cambridge University Press, 2012), p. 112.

most pernicious version is probably that in Russia, where there is an unholy alliance between the Kremlin and the Russian Orthodox Church, a proper Caesaropapism. The Russian government has been able to leverage support by appealing to Christian nationalist sympathies in other parts of Europe and America, by feeding audiences an explicit focus on culture-war questions related to LGBTQ+ issues. Here, we have to ask some painful questions. Is Patriarch Kirill just a black-hatted and bearded version of American moral-majority founder Jerry Falwell, albeit with incense? Is Vladimir Putin (an ex-KGB officer) and his invasion of Ukraine any more legal than George H. Bush (an ex-CIA official) and his invasion of Panama? To be fair, we wouldn't call them exact equations. We'd take Bush over Putin any day. But there are some disconcerting similarities between US imperialism and Russian aggression. Little wonder that the far right of US politics has been either critical of US support for Ukraine or fawning over Putin for defending a Christian empire.[38]

Christian nationalism is impoverished as it seeks a kingdom without a cross. It pursues a victory without mercy. It acclaims God's love of power rather than the power of God's love. We must remember that Jesus refused those who wanted to 'make him king' by force just as much as he refused to become king by calling upon 'twelve legions of angels'.[39] Jesus needs no army, arms or armoured cavalry to bring about the kingdom of God. As such, we should resist Christian nationalism as giving a Christian facade to nakedly political, ethnocentric and impious ventures.

Against civic totalism

One danger is the slow and steady accession of a soft authoritarianism under the guise of being 'progressive'.[40] We have in mind what

---

38 See Katherine Kelaidis, *Holy Russia? Holy War? Why the Russian Church is backing Putin against Ukraine* (London: SPCK, 2023), pp. 114–17.

39 John 6:15; Matthew 26:53.

40 What follows largely summarises Michael F. Bird, *Religious Freedom in a Secular Age: A Christian case for liberty, equality, and secular government* (Grand Rapids, MI: Zondervan, 2022), pp. 85–94.

happens when a state seeks to regulate as much of the individual's beliefs, convictions, conscience and religion as possible. A system where non-state-centric forms of life are corroded by constant surveillance and deliberate over-regulation.[41] What alerts us to this danger is several things:

1 emphases on a hierarchy of 'identities' rather than the rule of law and equality before the law to negotiate relationships between citizens;
2 adoption of a mode of moral reasoning that assigns all people into the binary slots of either 'oppressor' or 'oppressed';
3 legal preference for bespoke notions of 'equality' rather than accommodating religious and cultural differences;
4 the State conceived no longer as an instrumental good, but as an ultimate power with jurisdiction over every facet of life, in order to achieve a comprehensive renovation of society according to the State's progressive vision.

In other words, we are concerned about a progressive post-liberal order that does not value the right to dissent, the value of ideological diversity or the necessity of public debate, and that does not tolerate religions it cannot dictate to.[42] A political settlement where the State regards freedoms as permissible to the extent that they accord with the ever-changing wave of political progressivism. We fear a progressive post-liberal state that rejects liberalism's tenets on free speech, political pluralism, individualism and multiracial equality, while also rejecting socialist ideals of universal human experience, and the healing of ethnic and class divisions. Some species of political progressivism amount to liberationist sentiments without liberalism, a post-colonial project which does not end caste systems so much as reinvent them. There is danger in an aggressive

---

41 Luke Bretherton, *Christ and the Common Life: Political theology and the case for democracy* (Grand Rapids, MI: Eerdmans, 2019), p. 37.
42 Rex Ahdar and Ian Leigh, *Religious Freedom in the Liberal State*, 2nd edn (Oxford: Oxford University Press, 2013), pp. 17–19; Jeffrey Stout, *Democracy and Tradition* (Princeton, NJ: Princeton University Press, 2005), p. 299.

collectivism which argues that persons should not be treated as individuals who are equal before the law so much as expressions of specific sexual and ethnic identities. The result is a state that invests religious energy into its own icons and living saints, that punishes dissent from its own narratives,[43] that finds oppression everywhere except in itself and its system, that rewrites history as the history of group identities in perpetual and unending conflict, and that champions ethnic and sexual diversity while eliminating ideological diversity.[44]

Western democracies on the centre left are in danger of turning their countries into a 'bobocracy': rule by the 'bohemian bourgeois'.[45] These 'bobos' are a group of mostly white, rich and upper-middle-class elites in politics, the media and influencer professions with niche progressive values. The bobos often exhibit a deep resentment towards the working class and their pastimes, pieties and penchant for populist rather than paternal leaders.[46] The danger posed by the bobos is more than big government and empty virtue-signalling. It is government consciously committed to a radical sociopolitical project of attempting to redefine what it means to be a human being and the relationship of citizens to the State.

Many political progressives see Christianity as *the* number-one enemy against which they are struggling. As such, Christian communities, institutions, cultural influence and moral vision are the darkness against which their post-religious enlightenment is intended to shine. Christianity's influence can only be eliminated

---

43 As I write this, the Queensland government in Australia is proposing legislation that would compel clinicians and medical professionals to prioritise 'public confidence' in safety over the actual 'health and safety of the public'. In other words, a government could impose penalties on health professionals who say anything that is out of step with whatever the government of the day says about treating gender dysphoria or the risks associated with vaccines. This is an instance of a government deliberately politicising medicine rather than leaving best practice and advice to medical bodies and health professionals.

44 See Yascha Mounk, *The Identity Trap: A story of ideas and power in our time* (London: Penguin, 2023).

45 See David Brooks, *Bobos in Paradise: The new upper class and how they got there* (New York: Simon & Schuster, 2001).

46 See Paul Embery, *Despised: Why the modern left loathes the working class* (Cambridge: Polity, 2020); and Matthew Goodwin, *Values, Voice and Virtue: The new British politics* (London: Penguin, 2023). While both books apply principally to the British context, they are eminently translatable to wider Anglo-European political theatres.

by realigning institutions towards a secularised morality, by narrowing the parameters of religious freedom, by a coercive catharsis of religion itself, and by deconstructing resident fixtures such as history, constitutional law and even family. In the end, the progressive political vision amounts to what US political philosopher Stephen Macedo calls *civic totalism*, where the State is invested with all power and seeks to regulate as much of public and private life as possible.[47]

Civic totalism has forerunners in various political models in which individual rights are subordinate to the objectives of the State, and in which the necessity of crafting citizens into a certain mould trumps constitutional freedoms.[48] The primary contributor to modern visions of civic totalism is probably the philosopher and educational theorist John Dewey,[49] who believed that the state should sanction a scientifically informed public morality which made comprehensive claims to truth. Such a morality would be wide-ranging in the sense of including the public and private sphere. It would be rooted in the state education system, require the subordination of the Church to the state, and would even dissolve traditional religions in order to enable religious energies to be transferred to the advancement of state objectives. In the end, Dewey's political project envisaged a society unified around what Macedo labels 'a progressive democratic religion'.[50]

A central tenet of civic totalism is the view that public institutions are supreme and civil society is reduced to a legal fiction where liberties are granted, modified and revoked as the State determines. In addition, the distinctions between public and private spheres increasingly shrink. As a result, private life is treated as an artificial construct and is no longer regarded as an impenetrable frontier with inalienable privileges. For political progressives, the health of

---

47 Stephen Macedo, *Diversity and Distrust: Civic education in a multicultural democracy* (Cambridge, MA: Harvard University Press, 2003).

48 William A. Galston, *Practice of Liberal Pluralism* (Cambridge: Cambridge University Press, 2005), pp. 23–40.

49 Macedo, *Diversity and Distrust*, pp. 139–45.

50 Macedo, *Diversity and Distrust*, p. 142.

the State depends on a convergence of private and public values, requiring government to be empowered with the 'ability to turn people's deepest convictions – including their religious beliefs – in directions that are congruent with the ways of a liberal republic'.[51]

Consequently, religion, within civic totalism, is regarded as dangerous, since religion ascribes notions of ultimacy to something other than the State and the State's vision for the public good. Tyrants such as Herod, Nero or any contemporary example always fly into fits of rage when they hear rumours of 'another king' to whom people are paying homage.[52] For civic totalists, the danger of religion is that it creates a competing social vision and an alternative morality, which divides the loyalty of citizens away from the State's objectives for human conduct, rendering certain forms of religion as hostile to the State's ambitions.[53] In civic totalism, religion is permitted, but it is either a state-approved religion, or else, and more to the point, politics *is* the religion. In a godless age there are still gods, but people's religious energy and their worshipping proclivities are translated into the political arena.[54] Civic totalists are irreligious only for the reason that they have found new outlets for religious devotion, a devotion which is directed towards them, and which they believe demands mandatory participation.[55] As such, in civic totalism, the ruling regime must be protected by 'a shared account of basic civic values that impose limits on what

---

51 Macedo, *Diversity and Distrust*, p. 43.

52 Matthew 2:1–10; Acts 17:7.

53 Peter Leithart (*Against Christianity* [Moscow, ID: Canon Press, 2002], p. 136) writes: 'As soon as the church appears, it becomes clear to any alert politician that worldly politics is no longer the only game in town. The introduction of the church into *any* city means that the city has a challenger within its walls.'

54 French political philosopher Bernard-Henri Lévy (*The Testament of God* [New York: Harper & Row, 1980]) warned long ago of the 'cult of the political' (p. xii) and 'a religion of politics' (p. 21).

55 Lévy (*The Testament of God*, p. 35) observes how 'in fact, contrary to received opinion, the real theocrats are always recruited elsewhere, from among the murderers of God rather than his worshippers . . . Marx and Nietzsche, who executed Christ only in order to realise him more fully, to resurrect him everywhere, in the body of the new man, on the ruins of the end of history or those of the eternal return, were also theocrats. The terrorists of Germany and Italy, who chant "Neither God nor master" only in the name of a holier God, a more divine master, a superstitious law whose text they tattoo and machine-gun on the flesh of their victims, are also theocrats.'

can be true in the religious sphere'.[56] In this vein, the German philosopher Jürgen Habermas contended that the 'consciousness of the faithful' must be 'modernised' and forced to acquiesce and accept 'the individualistic and egalitarian nature of the laws of the secular community'.[57] This is not just religion within the limits of reason, but religion within the limits of the progressive vision of what religion is permitted to be, believe and behave.

There is no country or jurisdiction that one could clearly diagnose as 'civic totalist' in the fully orbed sense as we have described it. However, there are a frightful number of cultural figures and a lot of political rhetoric that certainly demonstrate people wanting to move in such a direction. It is not hard to imagine a clique of political intelligentsia who would love to have unfettered power to implement their totalising vision for how to make society a utopia on earth starting tomorrow. In addition, what is as demonstratable as it is disconcerting is that many Western democracies have increasingly engaged in more government-based religious discrimination and deliberately diminished international standards of religious freedom in comparison with countries in Asia, Africa and Latin America. This is an attempt to reduce or redefine religious freedom according to secular orthodoxies.[58] Sadly, the post-liberal ethos of the bobos requires adopting civic totalism or something very much like it to establish the unrivalled supremacy of the State to govern public and private spheres, to overrule conscience, to indoctrinate its views without question, and to even change religions.

There is something terrifying about a state so convinced of its own self-righteousness, that excites its citizens into a frenzy of rage and worship, a state that feels free to control, coerce and kill, all in

---

56 Macedo, *Diversity and Distrust*, p. 37.

57 Jürgen Habermas, 'Intolerance and Discrimination', *International Journal of Constitutional Law* 1.1 (2003): 2, 6.

58 Jonathan Fox, *Thou Shalt Have No Other Gods before Me: Why governments discriminate against religious minorities* (Cambridge: Cambridge University Press, 2020), which is based on a study of religious minorities in 183 countries between 1990 and 2014. See also Steven D. Smith, *The Rise and Decline of American Religious Freedom* (Cambridge, MA: Harvard University Press, 2014).

the name of its empire, for the sake of progress, or to prove it is on the 'right side of history'. As Lévy cautions:

> I fear nothing so much as a state which mobilizes, inflames the hearts of its subjects, dispenses them from the trouble of thinking, and then one fine day leads them like sleepwalkers along the paths of glory and concentration camps.[59]

The danger of post-liberal progressivism is that it turns into a secular type of Puritanism for people who have never read works by John Locke or Thomas Paine about tolerance and individual rights.[60]

The peculiar thing is that the Western 'culture wars' between progressives and conservatives are really in-house debates in a post-Christendom context about Christian ideas. That is precisely why many Christians don't map neatly onto the conservative versus progressive political dichotomy![61] Whether we are debating environmental care, a colonial legacy, women's autonomy over their own bodies, police brutality against people of colour, or rights for sexual minorities, these are concerns that emerge from a specifically Christian world view. The idea that the victim has sacred status does not derive from Islam, Hinduism, Buddhism or the Russian Revolution: it is as Christian as the Eucharist, crucifixes and baptisms at dawn. The fact is that so-called 'social-justice warriors' have much in common with sixteenth-century Puritans in their effort to purify society with a certain vision of public morals and to compel the Crown (the UK) or the White

---

59 Lévy, *The Testament of God*, pp. 36–7.

60 See Andrew Doyle, *The New Puritans: How the religion of social justice captured the Western world* (London: Constable, 2022), which is an acerbic critique of the progressive social-justice movement. It is one we do not endorse, but it shows the religious texture in so-called social-justice movements and their willingness to trade off civil rights for implementing their vision of social change.

61 It is also why we need to heed Klaus Bockmuehl's warning from 1980: 'Evangelicalism today, as it becomes aware of its social responsibility, must not accommodate itself to the trends of the day, either of the right or of the left. Instead, repentance and conversion are needed so that God is understood and accepted again as the reigning factor in the lives of individuals and society. Evangelicalism today must flee ideological dependence and formulate a social ethic informed by holy Scripture.' Klaus Bockmuehl, *The Challenge of Marxism: A Christian response* (Downers Grove, IL: InterVarsity Press, 1980), p. 165.

House (the USA) to acquiesce to the spiritual authority of the 'Church'. Swap out 'Church' for social advocacy movements such as #BlackLivesMatter, #ExtinctionRebellion, #MeToo and it's the same thing in a new garb. The fact that those movements regard themselves as possessing a divine-like mission, based on preventing harms, ending injustices and removing fears, underscores precisely their Christian qualities. For it is perfectly Christian to love one's gay or trans neighbour, to cry 'Let justice roll on like a river', to sing 'In his name all oppression shall cease' and to believe one exists in a covenant with creation/earth.

Tom Holland argues that the moral disputes at the heart of our culture are between rival versions of Christian ethics that are playing out in the conservative versus progressive divide. The problem is that only one side of the culture wars is aware that its argument functions within Christian grammar. It is fiercely ironic then that the secular *Kulturkampf* is really a critique of Christian ideas with other Christian ideas. Hence G. K. Chesterton's complaint that 'the modern world is full of old Christian virtues gone mad. The virtues have gone mad because they have been isolated from each other and are wandering alone.'[62] Western liberalism, with its talk of rights and aversion to injustice, is Christianity's prodigal son squandering his inheritance on 'disordered loves', while claiming it has inherited nothing from its parents.[63] It is a comic irony that the secular State has an innate inability to realise the ideals of love and justice taught by Jesus precisely because they believe such ideals must be attained without him! Yet the pulpit-pounding preacher and the irreligious professor are all attempting to tune their moral compasses after crawling out of a crater created by Jesus and his gospel.[64] Progressives need to understand that we have all internalised the Christian

---

62 G. K. Chesterton, 'The Suicide of Thought', in *G. K. Chesterton: The Dover reader* (New York: Dover, 2014), p. 271.

63 James K. A. Smith, *Awaiting the King: Reforming public theology* (Grand Rapids, MI: Baker, 2017), pp. 17, 112, 201.

64 See O'Donovan, *Desire of the Nations*, p. 212.

revolution and we are all riffing off the ethics of Jesus of Nazareth and his followers whether we care to admit it or not.[65]

Post-liberal progressives need to learn that one does not burn down the village (political rights and freedoms) in order to save the village from the barbarians (uneducated, religious or rural people who are not progressive). The crusade to restrict freedoms of speech, association, conscience and religion in order to prevent certain deplorable people from exercising the aforesaid freedoms is not going to end well. Sure, limiting the freedoms of your political rivals sounds terrific, as long as your political tribe remains permanently in power. But the erasure of liberties will come back to haunt you when political power lands in the hands of another political tribe, one that is perhaps nefarious, nationalistic and nakedly undemocratic. Then you will be wishing for limits on state power and the general freedom of the citizenry. Governments need a separation of powers, legislative checks and balances, and laws legislated as if the party or person we fear the most will acquire the power to wield them.

An alternative to civic totalism is a healthy account of human rights and responsibilities rooted in something more stable and enduring than the ever-progressing outrage of a vocal minority. Now for Christians, the common good, with ideas such as 'human rights', is not defined by an ephemeral 'social contract' drawn up in a religious vacuum. Rather, as Jamie Smith observes, the 'index and criterion for justice and the right ordering of society is not some generic, universal, or "natural" canon but rather the revealed, biblical story unfolded in God's covenant relationship with Israel and the church'.[66] Such an index has been impressed into historical documents which have articulated human rights as part of a moral exegesis of Western civilisation. The *Universal Declaration of Human Rights* (1948) enunciates these rights, which were described

---

65 This is the main thesis of Holland, *Dominion*. Note too Smith (*Awaiting the Kingdom*, pp. 93–4), who believes that the task of 'political theology' is 're-narrating to late modern liberal societies their religious and theological inheritance'.

66 Smith, *Awaiting the King*, p. 60.

by Pope John Paul II as 'a real milestone on the path of the moral progress of humanity'.[67] Likewise, the *International Covenant on Civil and Political Rights* (1966) sets out human rights to life, freedom of religion and conscience, freedom of speech, freedom of assembly and association, voting, due legal process and equality before the law. The notion that such rights can be diminished, denied or derogated by a particular progressive faction that demands to be unchallenged because of its own self-assured sense of being 'on the right side of history' must be dismissed. True, there are limits to religious freedom and freedom of speech. However, if we are to maintain the liberalism of a liberal democracy, there must always be limits to the limits we put on basic rights.[68]

Although a multicultural and liberal democracy will be conflictual – there are going to be different views on the common good, different solutions to political and economic problems, bitter arguments over sex and end-of-life issues – the resolution to any conflict is managing differences within diversity in a way that is equitable, charitable and proportionate. As one Canadian provincial court declared:

> A society that does not admit of and accommodate differences cannot be a free and democratic society – one in which its citizens are free to think, to disagree, to debate and to challenge the accepted view without fear of reprisal. This case [*Trinity Western University v. The Law Society of British Columbia*] demonstrates that a well-intentioned majority acting in the name of tolerance and liberalism, can, if unchecked, impose

---

67 John Paul II, Address to the 34th General Assembly of the United Nations, 2 October 1979, para. 7: https://www.vatican.va/content/john-paul-ii/en/speeches/1979/october/documents/hf_jp-ii_spe_19791002_general-assembly-onu.html (accessed 28 September 2023).

68 In international law, these are laid out in the Siracusa principles on when and how human rights can be temporarily suspended or modified. On the folly of imagining oneself 'on the right side of history', see N. T. Wright, *History and Eschatology: Jesus and the promise of natural theology* (Waco, TX: Baylor University Press, 2019), ch. 3, esp. pp. 85–7.

its views on the minority in a manner that is in itself intolerant and illiberal.[69]

The civic totalist ambitions of the bobos are not as directly confrontational as those of Fascist or Communist regimes. The elite class's inability to accept the notion of difference and dissent, combined with anxieties over the perceived disloyalties of the working class, an antipathy towards people of faith, and a desperate need to silence critics, lends itself to a sinister soft authoritarianism that could easily morph into something potentially Orwellian. Civic totalists attempt to subordinate the nation, family, religion and individuals beneath their ideology. In defiant response, the Church, as it defends its own freedom of worship and witness, must also stand for the liberties of others.[70] Laura Alexander acknowledges that the 'purpose of the state is to promote human well-being by providing order, protection, and the material and social goods that allow people to live reasonably stable lives and pursue good and meaningful ends', but she adds the important caveat that

> the state is not itself an ultimate end to be pursued, or an ultimate authority that merits people's highest loyalty. States' promotion of their interests, and their use of sovereign power, remain subject to critique from a higher moral plane.[71]

Those who acclaim Jesus as King will always be suspicious of a state or class that 'claims to be [a mediator] of ultimacy'.[72] Christians thus need to stand up to defend themselves and others, knowing that the

---

69 *Trinity Western University* v. *The Law Society of British Columbia*, 2016 BCCA 423 (CanLII), #193, http://www.canlii.org/en/BC/BCca/doc/2016/2016BCca423/2016BCCA423.html (accessed 11 September 2023).

70 *Centesimus Annus* (1991), §45.

71 Laura E. Alexander, 'Christian Realism and the State as Idol: Feminist and Postcolonial Critique and Christian Realist Theology in an Interdependent World', *Political Theology* 22 (2021): 682.

72 Smith, *Awaiting the King*, p. 79.

threat to one group's civil liberties, whether lesbians or Muslims, is a threat to everyone's.

Gospel *resistance* against *resurgent* empires

Every church, whether in Nigeria or Nicaragua, in Uzbekistan or the United States, must address injustice, oppression and tyranny, and seek to discern its calling to be a city on a hill. That is not to reduce the Church to a social action network, or to align it too closely with one political faction. It is to affirm what we know to be intuitively true, that our evangelical convictions about God putting the world to rights are only as strong as the evils we tolerate. So, whether we are resisting racism, illegal land seizures or a government controlled by gambling lobbyists, corruption and censorship, we must ask whether the governing bodies deserve our obedience, our dissent, our civil disobedience or our uncivil disobedience. This is no academic question but an in-your-face decide-right-now issue for Christians in many parts of the world. For instance, consider those Christians in Hong Kong who have taken different paths on how to respond to the government's repressive measures, as Kwok Pui-Lan describes:

> Christians organised prayer meetings in churches, public spaces, and in front of government buildings. Unlike public protests, religious meetings enjoy more protection from interference from the police, and the organisers do not have to apply for a permit to gather in public. Christians sang hymns and offered prayers for the city and for government officials and elected representatives. The Christian hymn 'Sing Hallelujah to the Lord' emerged as a unifying anthem during the early stage of the protests, sung by Christians and non-Christians alike. Some churches near the protest routes opened their doors and offered hospitality to protesters. But there were also Christians who believed in separation of Church and State, and that Christians should obey the authorities. Many evangelical

churches did not want to become politically involved and see evangelism as their priority. These divergent opinions have split local churches and denominations, with some members leaving their local churches because of their dissatisfaction with their churches' response to the protests.[73]

So how do we live, love, pray, work and follow Jesus Christ under the shadow of governments that deny citizens basic freedoms, manufacture idolatries and injustice, and act with impunity in their crimes against humanity? The answer is that faith is our defiance, and defiance is contagious. What is more, this is a faith working through love, faith in action, faith in a power higher than the powers who do evil. It is faith in a God who will bring the wicked to judgement and smash the thrones of evildoers.

As to what this looks like in action, the Church and those who commit themselves to walk in the way of Jesus Christ must be known for what they are for, but occasionally for what they are against. As Christians, we stand against Fascists and Communists; we must show solidarity with oppressed people, such as the brave Hongkongers and Ukrainians, as they discern in the precincts of their own consciences how to resist the oppressive and brutal actions of authoritarian states who either tyrannise over them or assault them with violence. Against Christian national-ism, we must stand against political movements in the USA or elsewhere that take the name of Christ in vain through a syn-cretic blend of nationalism, white supremacy and civil religion. Against civic totalists, we refuse to forfeit our freedoms to Stat-ist projects, we refuse to subordinate the rights of one identity to another identity, but demand instead the equality of everyone before the law. Remember, the greatest evils are not done by peo-ple who believe that what they do is wicked, but by those who be-lieve that what they do is righteous! In the face of such hate all too assured of its moral justification, followers of Jesus must deploy

---

73 Kwok Pui-Lan, *Postcolonial Politics and Theology: Unraveling empire for a global world* (Philadelphia, PA: Westminster John Knox, 2021), p. 126.

prayer and protests and sacred subversion against those who wish to erase or persecute the kulaks, the queers, Catholics, Jews, Palestinians, mestizos, refugees or even Christians in the name of security or to the delight of an ethno-religious majority.

Jesus is the great liberator. Jesus came 'to proclaim freedom for the prisoners'[74] so that we will 'know the truth, and the truth will make [us] free'.[75] Or as Paul said, 'The Messiah set us free so that we could enjoy freedom!'[76] and 'where the spirit of the Lord is, there is freedom!'[77] The German theologian Ernst Käsemann, who grew up during the Nazi regime, and theologically matured during the East versus West cold war, noted that 'the earth has no scarcity of lords, and they all demand obedience'. Yet for the disciple of the crucified Nazarene, 'Jesus' gift is Christian freedom and we live by that gift and grace of his, Christian freedom demands that we prove it on earth before it is perfected in heaven'. That freedom is proved by our love for others and the lords whom we choose to serve or to resist. For in the end:

the call of freedom has been sounded. It concerns every one of us personally, in our place, in our humanity, in this world of ours. The answer to it is the community of the free, and therefore the dawn of a new creation.[78]

---

74 Luke 4:18 (NIV).

75 John 8:32. Following O'Donovan, *Desire of the Nations*, pp. 146, 151.

76 Galatians 5:1.

77 2 Corinthians 3:17.

78 Ernst Käsemann, *Jesus Means Freedom* (Philadelphia, PA: Fortress, 1969), pp. 155–6.

7

Liberalism and Love in a Time of Fear and Fragmentation

Church and State revisited

Vincent Bacote notes that a political theology is trying to answer a couple of basic but important questions: 'Can there be Christian faithfulness in the public realm? If politics refers to our lives as citizens, then what does it mean to be Christian and a citizen of a county, state, country or world?'[1] Those indeed are the questions that Christians must wrestle with and, no surprise, Christians answer them in different ways. On the first part, Anabaptists and Anglicans have very different ideas about whether Christians can serve in public office. We have unreservedly taken an affirmative answer to that question. In fact, Christian faith is meant to be a public faith, for the common good, which compels us to do good, to make good, and to build good in private and public endeavours. As for the answer to the second question, we are compelled to be Christians for the sake of our municipality, state, country and even for the world. The problem is that the world is a difficult and dangerous place, more obviously so in the 2020s than any time since the 1930s, with economic upheaval, wars raging and visceral political divisions. So, if we must ascertain precisely how Christians relate to the State, we need to explore a few items further. In our political theology, we need to ask:

---

1 Vincent E. Bacote, *The Political Disciple: A theology of public life* (Grand Rapids, MI: Zondervan, 2015), p. 14.

1 How does God's authority relate to the authority of the State?
2 What type of state should Christians support?
3 How should Christians manage differences within the diversity
   of the state they find themselves a part of?

God's authority and the authority of the State

By what authority does the State do anything? The answer to that question depends entirely on whom you ask. There's everything from the divine right of kings to the dictatorship of the proletariat and a lot of other options in between. On a theological account, we could reason that government takes its legitimacy from God. God is the maker of heaven and earth, who raises up kings and empires, who directs the affairs of government through divine providence, who gives us government as a feature of common grace. As we saw earlier in the book, the apostles Paul and Peter both affirm the State's divinely given authority and the necessity of obedience to the State:

> Every person must be subject to the ruling authorities. There is no authority, you see, except from God, and those that exist have been put in place by God. As a result, anyone who rebels against authority is resisting what God has set up, and those who resist will bring judgement on themselves. For rulers hold no terrors for people who do good, but only for people who do evil.
>
> If you want to have no fear of the ruling power, do what is good, and it will praise you. It is God's servant, you see, for you and your good. But if you do evil, be afraid; the sword it carries is no empty gesture. It is God's servant, you see: an agent of justice to bring his anger on evildoers. That is why it is necessary to submit, not only to avoid punishment but because of conscience.
>
> That, too, is why you pay taxes. The officials in question are God's ministers, attending to this very thing. So pay each of

them what is owed: tribute to those who collect it, revenue to
those who collect it. Respect those who should be respected.
Honour the people one ought to honour.
(Romans 13:1–7)

Be subject to every human institution, for the sake of the Lord:
whether to the emperor as supreme, or to governors as sent by
him to punish evildoers and praise those who do good. This,
you see, is God's will. He wants you to behave well and so to
silence foolish and ignorant people. Live as free people (though
don't use your freedom as a veil to hide evil!), but as slaves of
God. Do honour to all people; love the family; reverence God;
honour the emperor.
(1 Peter 2:13–17)

The takeaway is that almost any government is better than anarchy.
God gives government as a gift to humanity to bring welfare, safety,
order and justice to human communities.[2] When government performs its job well it enables freedom to flourish, perpetuates peace
and administers justice. Whether we are talking about villages, whole
societies or mega-cities, we need collective government, otherwise
our way of life descends into lawlessness, and in lawlessness might
always makes right. The role of government is, as Calvin com-
mented, 'to provide for the common safety and peace of all' and 'to
preserve the tranquillity of the dominion, to restrain the seditious
stirrings of restless men. To help those forcibly oppressed, to punish
evil deeds'.[3] That explains why the State should be obeyed. The State
is from God and for our good. Now – as we've canvassed earlier –
the State should not be blindly obeyed. That is because the type of
authority that the State possesses is neither ultimate nor infallible.

The State exists for the purpose of exercising 'authority', but
that authority is derivative, not definitive. If anarchy is one possible problem that government solves, absolutism is the kind of

2 See also Proverbs 8:15; 21:1; Daniel 2:21.
3 Calvin, *Institutes* 4.20.9, 11.

Liberalism and Love in a Time of Fear

problem government can create.[4] Following Wolterstorff, we'd aver that state authority is not an ultimate position but a performance, an authorisation, permission to have power, a certain kind of power with limits. The implication of Romans 13:1–7 and 1 Peter 2:13–17 is that governing authority is conferred by God and therefore accountable to God. God alone *is* authority; consequently, states and their delegates merely *have* authority. The State is a divine servant to Almighty God irrespective of whether the State recognises it or not. The State answers to God as the God who appointed it to its task. The contrast is between God's absolute divine power and human government as a transient and terrestrial divine servant, that is, as a delegate bearing divine authority upon earth.[5]

Yet almost nobody today talks as if the State is a divine servant, is accountable to God, or exercises divine authority in its governance. There is a reason for that, a back story that has led to suspicion about anyone claiming to have divine sponsorship, to have 'God on our side' and a monopoly on the divine legitimacy. Whether or not we have experienced it for ourselves, we all fear the kind of theocracy in which certain humans are regarded, even if only by themselves, as infallible mouthpieces of the divine will.

In Christendom, the State was considered a divinely arranged social order where people were united in a common geography, ethnicity, religion and morality. The various classes or spheres of society each recognised that they had a duty to God and to one another. God had anointed kings and appointed them to rule, wisely and benevolently, over their subjects. But Christendom's concord was broken down by the awful malevolence of absolute monarchy, the terrors of empire, the rise of religious diversity, the Reformation, the Enlightenment, legal evolutions towards individual rights, the rise of nation states, the conflict between capital and workers' rights, as well as the legacy of colonial injustices. Christendom had such a traumatic experience of absolute monarchy that it had to

---

4   Peter Jensen, 'The Need for Good Politics', *The Global Anglican* 137 (2023): 101.

5   Nicholas Wolterstorff, *The Mighty and the Almighty: An essay in political theology* (Cambridge: Cambridge University Press, 2012), pp. 47–52, 116.

deconstruct its faith and dismantle the religious apparatus of the State.

The rejection of Christendom as a royal–priestly alliance had instant political effects. Instead of 'God save the king!' came 'Long live the republic!' It could be a God-fearing republic, but a republic it was. Truth be told, even constitutional monarchies are hardly different as they comprise a democratic parliamentarianism and a symbolic and titular head of state. In this post-Christendom settlement, authority was delegated not from on high, from God to the king, but transmitted from below, from people to public officials. Thus, governing actors, rather than trying to reflect heavenly authority in an earthly administration, now understood their objective as executing the will of the citizens as it applied to justice, security and welfare. Instead of 'the divine right of kings' (*jus divinum regum*) we have 'the voice of the people is the voice of God' (*vox populi, vox Dei*). Instead, of 'the King's Law' (*Rex Lex*) with absolute monarchy, we have 'the law is king' (*Lex Rex*) with the rule of law over kings and paupers alike. It is a fact that forcing the State to answer to its own citizens promotes transparency and accountability.

In a post-Christendom context, whether in a Communist state or in a democratic republic, God does not ordinarily enter into the conceptualisation of state authority. To reiterate, that has a historical basis. The limitations of divinely sanctioned despotism, even with a wise, benevolent and pious despot, were plain and self-evident. We are not convinced that Christian monarchies were the worst system of governance, given that the alternatives of the time were pagan tribal confederations, Islamic caliphates or being the vassal of Eurasian steppe armies. Still, it was not hard to improve upon Christendom. The downside of absolute monarchy, often propped up by a bishop declaring that to disobey the king was the same as disobeying God, was evident to a good many.

Be that as it may, Western liberal democracies, without the stability produced by a representative monarch or a shared meta-narrative, have always run the risk of fragmentation and republican fratricide. Mere opposition to a king, tsar or sultan does not unify a population for long if it is pregnant with ethnic, religious and class rivalries. The problem with state authority from below – and this is proving to be the key vulnerability of liberal democracies today – is that they must be rooted in some kind of consensus. Without a consensus about the nature of justice or a shared understanding of the common good, it is almost impossible to create social cohesion and political concord. Without some kind of shared social vision, what is considered 'good' becomes ephemeral, driven by fashion and theatrics, torn asunder by disparate groups, each with their own agenda. Without a shared story, we cease caring about the common good and allow our minds to be dulled by endless entertainment, we cease to have the ability to discern truth from lies, or we demand that all opposition is destroyed even if this overthrows our own freedoms. Without shared symbols, stories, ideals, goals and visions of human life together, a liberal democracy can fracture and fragment its freedoms away. Without belief in one who sits above the table of petty partisan squabbles, we are destined to be governed by grifters and torn apart by grievances.

Take heed. No democracy can survive external actors maliciously exploiting its internal fissures without a narrative substructure rooted in something beyond itself. Nor can a democracy withstand the temptations of plutocratic scheming or resist a demagogical erosion of civil liberties unless it has learned what those liberties are for. Democracy cannot survive without having a story about its struggle for freedom and the origins of its rights and duties, or without knowing the true purpose of human flourishing.

This is where the Christian story possesses acute political utility in setting forth a story where evil is real, where evil takes the form of empires, from Pharaoh to Caesar, where evils, the mundane and the menacing, can also take root in ourselves. The answer to evil is not revenge but redemption. When empires do their worst, God sets them aside with the divine revolutions of exodus and Easter. Indeed, the Eucharist is where we celebrate God's reign siding with the victims of empire, vindicating the people, and bringing victory over sin, death and evil. God conquers the despot lurking in all our hearts. In this story, the State is simultaneously a source of evil and a potential safeguard against it. Christians can argue that God authorises the State to effect a common good, that is, a specific vision of justice, security and welfare. Evidently, then, we can legitimately apply religious resources to think about topics pertaining to politics and power, authority and accountability, rights and responsibilities, constraints and freedoms.[6] For Christians, the common good is not rooted in the whim of mob mentality, slavishly tied to fickle fashions, limited to populism or plebiscites, or even attained in shared goals as banal as 'live and let live'. Authority is from God to the State and meets with the consensus of the people. The ultimate sin of government is not against law, tribe or house, but against the one who wills that government must govern justly, wisely and benevolently.

We are contending that an ideal state has its freedoms and obligations tethered to something transcendent yet translatable. A state anchored in a particular story with universal relevance. A state authority that knows it is not and never should try to be almighty, combined with a citizenry that aspires to civic virtue. In such a settlement, even with a secular constitution, one may appeal to sustaining traditions and narratives such as those supplied by religion to enable a comprehensive suite of freedoms and safeguards against tyranny and anarchy. A state that seeks to be just needs a coherent and compelling justification for the rights and responsibilities of its citizens which is rooted in something bigger than themselves and even beyond themselves. Also, such a state needs common convictions about who humans are, something like creatures bearing the 'image of God' who share 'one stock',[7] in other words, a political anthropology that explains universal human value. Such a state needs to provide its citizens with a summation of their agreed duties and obligations to one another as summed up in something like the Decalogue, the Sermon on the Mount, or the parable of the Good Samaritan, even if it then finds secular expression in various bills of rights and declarations about human rights. A state that creates

---

6   Wolterstorff, *The Mighty and the Almighty*, pp. 8–9.

7   Genesis 1:27; Acts 17:26.

citizens who are committed to cultivating common virtues such as love, fairness and equality. A state of this order is also in need of some kind of eschatology about the *telos*, the end or goal of freedom, felicity and flourishing. Although no religion should pursue hegemonic supremacy in a free state, religion can contribute to the basic questions of what the State should and should not do, the obligations of citizens and the purpose of the State itself.

In sum:

1 God gives authority to the State for the common good;
2 the State does not possess authority as much as it performs a divinely delegated task with authority;
3 the notion of a divinely delegated state authority as per Christendom was open to manifold abuses, hence the need for an authority that operates on the basis of the consensus of the governed;
4 the problem with stateship from below is that it becomes fragmented and fratricidal without a sustaining narrative or a supporting vision of the common good; therefore
5 Christians can insist that the State is neither infallible nor inviolable; it answers to God, and the stories and symbols of Jesus can furnish a republic or commonwealth with resources to forge bonds of civil affection and common purpose.

The Christian case for liberal democracy

One could argue that liberal democracy is Christendom 2.0, reloaded and reconfigured, attempting to deal with the failures and fissures of the pre-modern world. More specifically, Protestant Christians, convinced that all truth is God's truth, whether scientific or political, and that truth is universal, sought to export the gospel, science and constitutionalism wherever they went. Nobody believes it is 'self-evident that all men [and women] are created equal' unless they have read and been shaped by Genesis 1:27 about men and women in the 'image of God' and 'God loved the world . . .' from John 3:16. Human rights and religious pluralism have their deepest roots in countries formed by missional Protestantism.[8] Political liberalism, far from being the formidable foe of Christianity, proves in fact to be its lost child, who refuses to believe the truth about its paternity.

Liberal democracy is 'liberal' in the sense that it regards civic freedoms as an inherent good that should not be subject to limitation unless completely necessary, and it is 'democratic' in the sense that voting rights apply equally to all citizens and each citizen's vote should have the same weight. We write now neither to celebrate nor to castigate liberal democracy. Instead, we wish to prosecute the thesis that in a world with a human propensity for evil, greed and injustice, liberal democracy stands as the least worst option for human governance. Liberal democracy is neither a necessary nor a sufficient condition for a just society, but it can be an enabling condition for a just society.

It might be hard to accept or acknowledge this, but the truth is that Christians have not always been devoted to democracy. Eusebius declared his support for monarchy where 'there is one Sovereign, and his sovereign Word and Law is one', since God is one, not a plurality of divine powers. Monarchy, he claimed, was preferable to the democracy that brings only 'anarchy and disorder'.[9] Remarks such as that make one wonder whose side Eusebius would have taken in the 1930s. Turning now to John Calvin, we can see that he believed that God's providence permits a variety of governments with kings, senates and free states. According to Calvin,

---

8 There is much literature to consider here, including John Witte, *The Reformation of Rights: Law, religion and human rights in early modern Calvinism* (Cambridge: Cambridge University Press, 2007); Joan Lockwood O'Donovan, 'The Liberal Legacy of English Church Establishment: A theological contribution to the legal accommodation of religious plurality in Europe', *Journal of Law, Philosophy and Culture* 4 (2011): 14–75; Robert D. Woodberry, 'The Missionary Roots of Liberal Democracy', *American Political Science Review* 106 (2012): 244–74; Larry Siedentop, *Inventing the Individual: The origins of Western liberalism* (London: Penguin, 2015); James K. A. Smith, *Awaiting the King: Reforming public theology* (Grand Rapids, MI: Baker, 2017), pp. 91–150; esp. James Simpson, *Permanent Revolution: The Reformation and the illiberal roots of liberalism* (Cambridge, MA: Belknap, 2019).

9 Eusebius, *Speech for Thirtieth Anniversary of Constantine's Accession* 1, cited in *From Irenaeus to Grotius: A sourcebook in Christian political thought, 100–1625*, ed. Oliver O'Donovan and Joan Lockwood O'Donovan (Grand Rapids, MI: Eerdmans, 1999), p. 60.

the danger of monarchy was tyranny and the hazard of aristocracy was factionalism. Calvin's own preference for a civil governance was 'a compound of aristocracy and democracy'.[10] J. R. R. Tolkien, author of the *Lord of the Rings* trilogy, critiqued authoritarian regimes in his allegories of Isengard and Mordor, but in his 'Scourging of the Shire', we find Tolkien's implicit critique of the earth-scorching bureaucratisation that takes place in democracies.[11] Tolkien was in the end a Catholic eco-royalist who preferred a monarch acting as custodian of people and pastures to a democratic socialism with its bean counters, endless rules and regulations, and multiplication of committees. David Bentley Hart even labels Tolkien an 'anarcho-monarchist'.[12]

As we saw earlier, the early Christians, like the Jews of their day, were not particularly worried about *how* a ruler became a ruler (whether authority was inherited or acquired in a palace coup, by conquest or in revolution) but they were very concerned about how rulers behaved and what they did once they became rulers. History shows that there is no single political structure that Christianity is tied to as Christians have lived under and advocated for different types of government. Be that as it may, we can provide a Christian defence of liberal democracy, not as the only type of government Christians may wish to support, but perhaps the one that can be undergirded with the Christian vision, and which represents a type of 'wisdom' that will make the most of human endeavours.

Christianity and liberalism

We can provide a Christian justification for 'liberalism' through the notion of 'love of neighbour'.[13] In order to love our 'neighbour', we must allow our neighbour to be beside us and yet be different from us. Our neighbour has permission to be 'other' than us.

---

10 Calvin, *Institutes* 4.20.8.

11 See Bruno Bacelli, *How to Misunderstand Tolkien: The critics and the fantasy master* (Jefferson, NC: McFarland & Co., 2022), pp. 80, 89.

12 David Bentley Hart, *A Splendid Wickedness and Other Essays* (Grand Rapids, MI: Eerdmans, 2016), pp. 71–5.

13 See Leviticus 19:18; Matthew 5:43; 19:19; 22:39; Romans 13:9–10; Galatians 5:14; James 2:8.

That requires us permitting and even celebrating the freedom of others to find happiness, fulfilment, flourishing, purpose and meaning in ways that we might disagree with or disapprove of. Unless their happiness is to the direct detriment of our own, our neighbour is free to be who they are, how they are, where they there, whenever they are. Love of neighbour is a way to disrupt hierarchical, grievance-based, identity-ordered ways of assigning status.[14] The natural sequel is love of enemies,[15] and the best way to destroy our enemies is to make them our friends, our partners, our neighbours. If we add to that the parable of the Good Samaritan,[16] then we recognise that our neighbours, who are religiously and ethnically different from us, have the same capacity for goodness, love and mercy that we possess. We choose to affirm the freedom to be different and to accept other people's choices insofar as they are not detrimental to any other good. Liberalism means liberty to love despite our differences.[17] Liberalism prefers generosity over conformity. Liberalism chooses to find goodness in others.

Liberal democracies exhibit what William Galston calls *expressive liberty* which is a presumption in favour of individuals and groups living their lives as they see fit and according to their own understanding of what gives life meaning and value. In the liberal democratic State, the State must bear and discharge the burden of proof whenever it seeks to restrict expressive liberty.[18] This applies particularly to freedom of religion, freedom of conscience and freedom of political activism. Liberty is the norm, not the exception. Any curtailment of liberties must be exceptional rather than excessive, fairly distributed rather than targeted at particular

---

14 Luke Bretherton, *Christ and the Common Life: Political theology and the case for democracy* (Grand Rapids, MI: Eerdmans, 2019), p. 41.

15 Matthew 5:43–8.

16 Luke 10:25–37.

17 The question of course is: which differences make a difference? If my neighbour says that circumcising his daughters is part of his religion and culture, should that be permitted as 'diversity'? What are the limits for the toleration of diversity and what are the principles behind those limits?

18 William A. Galston, *Practice of Liberal Pluralism* (Cambridge: Cambridge University Press, 2005), pp. 2–3.

demographics. Change of public order must be consensual and disagreements resolved through persuasion rather than by deception or coercion.

The qualification we need to make is that the liberty in liberalism is neither absolute nor endless. The law exists to uphold liberty as much as to restrict it. That is because no person can be fully autonomous, a law unto themselves, without responsibility to others in their choices and actions. All rights have limitations, just as all freedoms come with responsibilities. If everyone did 'what was right in their own eyes' the results would be public anarchy, moral relativism and civic chaos.[19] Calvin reports a saying from the time of the Roman emperor Nerva: 'It is indeed a bad thing to live under a prince with whom nothing is lawful, but a much worse to live under one with whom all things are lawful.'[20] The ability to do anything and everything we desire is only good if that which we desire is good for ourselves and good for others. John Paul II's encyclical *Evangelium Vitae* points out the limitations of absolutely autonomy:

> If the promotion of the self is understood in terms of absolute autonomy, people inevitably reach the point of rejecting one another. Everyone else is considered an enemy from whom one has to defend oneself. Thus, society becomes a mass of individuals placed side by side, but without any mutual bonds. Each one wishes to assert himself independently of the other and in fact intends to make his own interests prevail.

To defuse a possible civil war among autonomous selves 'some kind of compromise must be found, if one wants a society in which the maximum possible freedom is guaranteed to each individual'.[21] The expressive individualism of liberalism then must be balanced with our obligations to protect the welfare of our fellow citizens.

---

19 Judges 17:6; 21:25.
20 Cited by Calvin, *Institutes* 4.20.10.
21 *Evangelium Vitae* (1995), §20.

Christianity and democracy

We can also engage in a form of Christian reasoning that allows us to make sense of, and even articulate the advantages of, democracy. One cannot prove democracy from the Bible any more than one can prove religious freedom, judicial independence or freedom of association. The Bible does not teach democracy in the same way that it teaches that Jesus is Lord, murder is wrong, and disciples should not act like unholy hooligans. We find in the Bible spasmodic accounts of leaders being appointed by popular consent, such as when Moses instructed the Hebrew tribes to choose leaders who were wise, discerning and reputable, and when the men of Judah anointed David as king over the house of Judah.[22] But the Christian Scriptures do provide some principles and a type of wisdom that suggest to us, who inhabit a civilisation shaped by the Christian revolution, that democracy is a desirable type of government. Democracy is somewhere between expedient and advantageous given the nature of human beings as sinful to the bone, and given that God's goal for human beings is to be part of covenantal communities filled with love for God and love for their neighbours. As Reinhold Niebuhr famously said, 'Man's capacity for justice makes democracy possible; but man's inclination to injustice makes democracy necessary.'[23]

The consent of the governed has always been an important facet of government. Even despots must descend from their thrones occasionally to gauge the word on the street about their reign and reputation. When Zadok anointed Solomon as king of Israel it was met with public acclamation: 'Long live King Solomon!'[24] The deacon Agapetos wrote to the Byzantine emperor Justinian in the sixth century: 'Count your kingdom safe when you rule with consent. An oppressed people rises up at the first opportunity, but one that is tied to its rulers by good will can be relied on to comply with

---

22 Deuteronomy 1:13–15; 2 Samuel 2:4.

23 Reinhold Niebuhr, *The Children of Light and the Children of Darkness: A vindication of democracy and a critique of its traditional defense* (New York: Scribner's, 1944), p. ix.

24 1 Kings 1:39.

government.'[25] This is why the US Declaration of Independence includes the assertion that, to safeguard political rights, 'governments are instituted among men, deriving their just powers from the consent of the governed'.[26] Theologians in the past have recognised that while all power is from God, the legitimation of that authority comes through the people.[27]

The limitations of democracies are obvious to those of us who have lived in them for long enough. Whether it is campaign donations, political careerism, nepotism, factionalism, legislative gridlock or media biases, there is much to complain about. One obvious problem with democracy is that power ends up in the hands of people who desperately want it. They want political power more for their own interests and ideology than for the common good. Even worse, the only way to remove one ambitious or incompetent politician is to replace them with a potentially more ambitious and even more incompetent politician.[28] The vulnerability of democracy to a slide into dictatorship is evident from how Hitler found a way to become the democratically elected chancellor of Germany in 1933, and then fused the office of president and chancellor to become Führer in 1934. The Czechoslovak Communist leader Klement Gottwald was democratically elected as prime minister in 1946 and then staged a coup d'état to become president in 1948, imposing a Stalinist model of governance. Democracy is only as good as the people and institutions guarding it.

Liberal democracy as safeguard against autocracy

To bolster the case for liberal democracy, it is useful to articulate the many benefits which it confers on its citizens, which we enumerate as follows:

25 Agapetos, *Heads of Advice* 35, cited in *From Irenaeus to Grotius*, ed. O'Donovan and O'Donovan, p. 185.
26 See Wayne Grudem, *Politics According to the Bible* (Grand Rapids, MI: Zondervan, 2010), pp. 106–9.
27 Jacques Ellul, *Anarchy and Christianity* (Grand Rapids, MI: Eerdmans, 1988), p. 29.
28 Hart, *Splendid Wickedness*, p. 72.

1 ***Individual rights.*** Liberal democracies enshrine individual rights and freedoms in either a constitution or a bill of rights. These rights pertain to freedoms of thought, commerce, speech, press, religion, association, voting, and to petition and protest. Such rights ensure that all members of society can freely express themselves and pursue their hopes and happiness without fear of reprisal.

2 ***Universal suffrage and participation.*** Liberal democracies enable and encourage political participation from all members of the citizenry, irrespective of their gender, ethnicity, religion or socio-economic status. Everyone can vote, run for public office and serve in the public administration. This ensures that all voices are heard, all parties and policies can be scrutinised, and elected officials are representative of the needs and desires of the constituency. The underlying principle is that government can only proceed with the consent of the governed.

3 ***Separation of powers.*** Liberal democracies recognise that no branch of government should have unqualified authority or unfettered power. As such, liberal democracies normally include executive, legislative and judicial branches of government. This separation of powers ensures that no branch of government is all-powerful. This is why the politicisation of a judiciary, and the partisanship of public servants, is a threat to democratic order.

4 ***Peaceful conflict resolution.*** Liberal democracies do carry an underlying tension, perhaps even a vulnerability, in that they promote individual freedom and yet such freedoms may conflict with varied perceptions of the common good. For example, a liberal democracy will undoubtedly have different ideas among citizens as to the extent and limitation of freedoms pertaining to gun ownership, reproductive choice, marriage, parental rights, separation of Church and State, and more. Democracies are compelled to tolerate and enfranchise people who stand in resolute opposition to the very idea of democracy itself. As a result, citizens are forced into deliberation, even ferocious debate, on these topics. Liberal democracy ideally provides mechanisms to balance competing rights and to debate the nature and extent of

liberties in a civil manner. Liberal democracy provides a frame-work for resolving disputes through peaceful means, such as a free press, persuasion, advocacy, elections and mediation. Liberal democratic states, then, do not have to resort to coercion, censorship or coups to resolve differences.

5 *Economic opportunity and equality.* Liberal democracies are often associated with freedom of commerce, the profit motive, and the ability to enjoy the benefits of one's own labours. Economic freedom leads to job creation, facilitates economic mobility, fosters innovation, and results in increased economic productivity. What is more, when economic opportunity is combined with a fair tax system, it ensures that the tax burden is evenly distributed. Liberal democracies attempt to manufacture economic growth while simultaneously ensuring that the taxation system and government programmes do not create a situation where the rich get richer and the poor get poorer, but the total wealth of the nation is shared among its citizens.

6 *Government transparency and accountability.* Liberal democracies hold elected officials and government institutions accountable to the people. This helps ensure that government policies are transparent and responsive to the needs of the people, and that corruption and abuse of power are eliminated.

7 *Rule of law and judicial independence.* The rule of law is a fundamental principle of liberal democracies. In practice, this means that no one person, not even those in power, is above the law. Everyone, especially those in public office or in public service, is held accountable for their actions. In addition, a separation of powers also safeguards abuses of authority as citizens have the right of appeal to an independent judiciary to protect them from abuses of government power. Accordingly, the rule of law requires judicial independence as magistrates are able to review the legislation and actions of government officials and hold them to the same standard as every other citizen. The judiciary is free of political interference and manipulation and is able to interpret the law without fear of reprisal. This is important as only an independent judiciary is able to make sure that

the law is applied fairly and impartially, and that all citizens are treated equally under the law.

8 **Self-critique.**[29] Civilisations with an emphasis on freedom and aversion to cruelty and tyranny are capable of sustaining self-critique. The first example of this is perhaps Euripides' plays *Trojan Women* and *Hecuba* which provide an implicit critique of Athenian imperialism with the exploitation and suppression of Athens' allies in the Delian league in the fifth century BC. The worst aspects of the British Empire were frequently met with denunciations by missionaries, clergy, activists and parliamentarians, who could use the benefits of a free press, parliamentary privilege or even the pulpit to decry the evils of their own country. While the Afghans, Persians and British ransacked and pillaged India in the eighteenth century, only the British literally put themselves on trial for doing so.[30] Liberal democracy does have a capacity for self-denunciation and thus self-correction. Such in-house critique is possible in a liberal democracy but impossible in an authoritarian nation.

The discussion above is admittedly Anglo-/Eurocentric. We need to consider how Christians in the majority world have related to governing authorities, and note the complicating factors in discrete locations caused by geography, history, colonialism, corruption, tribalism, sectarianism and religion that determine the political infrastructure.[31] Alas, Western liberalism might not be easily indigenised or parachuted into the non-Western settings where there is no conception of shared humanity, no tradition of individual rights, no concept of secularity, and no separation of powers. This is precisely why the attempts to turn parts of the Middle East and Central Asia into liberal democracies have either proved difficult or been

---

29 Sometimes, perhaps misleadingly, called 'oikophobia', which is critique of one's own house, society or culture.

30 See William Dalrymple, *The Anarchy: The relentless rise of the East India Company* (London: Bloomsbury, 2019), ch. 8.

31 Jonathan Cole, *Christian Political Theology in an Age of Discontent: Mediating Scripture, doctrine and political reality* (Eugene, OR: Wipf & Stock, 2019), pp. 1–2.

an abject failure. Or else, some countries, such as Turkey, Indonesia, Malaysia and India, are democracies, but they are not 'liberal' in the classic sense, as they are tied to ethno-religious civilisations that place firm limits on political, personal and religious liberties.[32] As such, local factors and immediate history have always shaped how churches have related to the state authorities and the models of government that they support in various parts of the world. Note, too, that over the centuries of church history, Greek Orthodox Christians and French Huguenots often preferred to live under Muslim Ottoman rule than under a Catholic king. Even today, Christians in Syria have sided with the Assad regime because of the horrors perpetrated against them by Sunni extremists. Sometimes it is a matter of siding with the lesser evil. Also, the Western preoccupation with individual rights and liberty, over, say, the common good and combating poverty, betrays a hierarchy of values and a particular social location which is neither self-evident to, nor expedient for, every other Christian church in the world. We cannot demand that everyone read Romans 13, remember Christendom, or think about building for, the kingdom with a Western mindset. We do well to heed the claim of T. S. Eliot: 'To identify any particular form of government with Christianity is a dangerous error for it confounds the permanent with the transitory, the absolute with the contingent.'[33]

Even so, there is nothing to stop us advocating and celebrating liberal democracy as one of the most noble achievements of human civilisation, an achievement that would not have happened, and is not even conceivable, apart from the Christian heritage of the West. There would never be human rights as self-evident truths without scriptural notions of the 'image of God' and the command to 'love your neighbour as yourself' as it was interpreted in Christian societies.[34] As Luke Bretherton notes, 'Christians do not need democracy to practice their faith, but democracy enshrines some central Christian commitments, and so, as a judgement of practical

---

32 On which, see Shadi Hamid, *The Problem of Democracy: America, the Middle East, and the rise and fall of an idea* (Oxford: Oxford University Press, 2022).

33 T. S. Eliot, *The Idea of a Christian Society* (London: Faber & Faber, 1939), p. 57.

34 Genesis 1:27; Leviticus 19:18.

reason, democracy should be an aspirational feature of political order for Christians.'[35]

We hasten to add that women and sexual minorities generally fare better in liberal democracies than in any rival or alternative systems of government. Refugees don't flee from liberal democracies, but they do flee to them.[36] In addition, every change of government without bloodshed, every inquiry that exposes government corruption, every journalistic report that demands action on police brutality, every citizen who wins an appeal against the government, shows that liberal democracy, though not necessarily perfect, is eminently preferable to a host of other types of government around the world.[37]

This is why we must defend our democracies from external interference, nefarious actors and internal combustion. A study of twentieth-century history shows that democracies can all too easily degenerate into hubs of racial hatred, oligarchy, plutocracy, crony-capitalism and dictatorship. We must be vigilant against free-market fundamentalism that exploits the poor and vulnerable, aggressive militarism that urges us to war, not peace, and escalating authoritarianism that tells us that diminishing our liberty is the only path to safety.[38] It does not normally happen overnight but takes place through a gradual and stealth-like erosion of democratic processes and institutions. It occurs when people have assumed that checks and balances would kick in, when people thought they could use some reprehensible group for their own end, only to discover themselves being used by them. Democracy falters when people take democracy for granted rather than prizing and cherishing the freedoms it gives us. Democracy can atrophy with apathy.

35 Bretherton, *Christ and the Common Life*, p. 12.

36 Cole, *Christian Political Theology*, p. 88.

37 We should remember that it was the Athenian democracy that had the Greek philosopher Socrates executed on charges of impiety and corrupting the youth. Democratic countries such as the UK and the USA have engaged in practices ranging from slavery, to conquest, to colonisation with the consent and enablement of politicians, business, media and the various classes. I say this because we can only regard democracy as the best way of constructing a human civilisation if we are prepared to wrestle with its historical failures and potential weaknesses.

38 Cornel West, *Democracy Matters: Winning the fight against imperialism* (New York: Penguin, 2005), ch. 6.

It happens when citizens refuse to be vigilant. Democracy dies when people refuse to speak and act . . . until it is too late. Theologian Kwok Pui-Lan, writing from the Hong Kong context, tells us about the warning signs that democracy is being undermined:

> The worrying signs that democracy was being undermined included sabotaging constitutions, sidelining legislative bodies in the name of representing the people, packing courts with loyalists, delegitimizing opponents and the election processes, attacking the free press, condoning or encouraging violence, and threatening to take legal action against political rivals.[39]

May it never happen to us. But that is the thing: it *can* happen to us if we are not alert and do not vigilantly guard our democracies. For, as Timothy Snyder writes, 'If none of us is prepared to die for freedom, then all of us will die under tyranny.'[40] To defend democracy, we must practise it. This means getting out to vote, taking a stand, helping a candidate, running as a candidate, scrutinising results, ensuring voting rights and eradicating gerrymanders. Above all, democracy means accepting that sometimes our preferred candidate loses. It means that political disappointment is better than having our own despot in power. We need to choose truth over tribe. Defend due process and institutions even if we find them cumbersome and conflictual. When it comes to change, we need the patience to play the long game, not go for the quick fix that is promised by the seductive words of a demagogue. Our greatest argument against tyranny, and the answer to the critics of liberal democracy, is to point to the monumental achievements of liberal democracy in improving the quality of life and preserving equality under the law for all its citizens. Beyond that, it falls to us to work tirelessly to make liberal democracies more liberal, more democratic, and further exemplifying the virtues of love, justice, equality and responsibility.

---

39 Kwok Pui-Lan, *Postcolonial Politics and Theology: Unraveling empire for a global world* (Philadelphia, PA: Westminster John Knox, 2021), p. 92.

40 Timothy Snyder, *On Tyranny: Twenty lessons from the twentieth century* (London: Crown, 2017), ch. 20.

Christians in a pluralistic and multicultural setting need to find unity in diversity, practise hospitality as a political discipline, and build for the kingdom by contributing to the common good of all.

The case for confident pluralism

In liberal democracies, the fact that people are free means that they will inevitably encounter diverse ideas about how to live an authentic, intentional and even spiritual life. How do we ensure a fair go for everyone? Free countries attract a diversity of people with diverse ideas precisely because people are free to disagree, dissent and debate. But therein lies the tension. Because diversity means conflict! A society of Baptists, agnostics, Muslims, atheists, conservatives, progressives, LGBTQ+, immigrants, rich, poor, all living together cheek by jowl, will breed an assortment of perspectives in terms of how society should be governed, what laws should be passed, and how to manage our differences. When diversity meets democracy, it always creates friction and frustration. How is a progressive, single, white, male, gay, vegan, anti-vaccine, pro-legalised-cannabis, pro-open-borders, atheist, working in hospitality, to live beside a conservative, black, Baptist, SUV-driving, bacon-loving, gender-critical stay-at-home mother of four? Democracy's strength is that it can sustain diversity. Democracy's weakness is that diversity creates conflict.

Liberal democracy only works if we find a way of living with differences, dealing with diversity, tolerating others, not begrudgingly, but in a manner that respects people's right to hold their opinion and pursue their social vision. One could respond to diverse perspectives by pursuing political homogeneity, making sure everyone votes one way, for one party, for one set of policies. But that requires compromising either the 'liberalism' or the 'democracy' in 'liberal democracy'. Unless we are going to bully people or break all dissent, we need to find a way of managing differences within our democratic diversity. It is here that we wish to commend a vision of political unity within social diversity by appeal to the concept of confident pluralism.[41] According to legal philosopher John Inazu:

> Confident pluralism offers a political solution to the practical problem of our differences. Instead of the elusive goal of *E pluribus unum* ['Out of many, one'], it suggests a more modest possibility – that we can live together in our 'many-ness.' That vision does not entail Pollyannish illusions that we will overcome our differences and live happily ever after. We will continue to struggle with those whose views we regard as irrational, immoral, or even dangerous. We are stuck with the good, the bad, and the ugly of pluralism. Yet confident pluralism remains possible in both law and society . . . Confident pluralism allows genuine differences to coexist without suppressing or minimizing our firmly held convictions. We can embrace pluralism precisely because we are confident in our own beliefs, and in the groups and institutions that sustain them.[42]

Confident pluralism has a very simple premise, namely, that people have the right to be different, to think differently, to live differently, to worship differently, without fear of reprisal. Confident pluralism operates with the idea that politics has instrumental rather than ul-timate value. In other words, politics is a means, not an end. No state, no political party, no leader is God-like, or can demand blind de-votion. Any attempt by political actors to create social homogeneity by compelling conformity, by bullying minorities or by punishing dissent, whether in religion or in policy, is anti-liberal and undem-ocratic. As Australian political leader Tim Wilson writes: 'A free society does not seek to homogenise belief or conscience but

---

41 See similarly Michael F. Bird, *Religious Freedom in a Secular Age: A Christian case for liberty, equality, and secular government* (Grand Rapids, MI: Zondervan, 2022), pp. 94–9.

42 John D. Inazu, *Confident Pluralism: Surviving and thriving through deep difference* (Chicago, IL: University of Chicago Press, 2016), pp. 6–7.

instead, affirms diversity and advocates for tolerance and mutual respect.[43]

We need confident pluralism, or something close to it, because liberal democracy creates a plurality of political perspectives. This plurality is messy and conflictual; it leads to confrontations and is not conducive to public unity, let alone social uniformity. The fact is that the consciences of some people will lead them to kneel for a national anthem, while others will proudly stand and place their hand on their heart. In such a diverse society, as Alasdair MacIntyre said, politics is 'civil war carried on by other means'.[44] The disparate and diverse beliefs that occupy the public square, parliaments, or even the food court plaza, mean that we need the practice of confident pluralism to enable us to respect differences rather than attempt to suppress or punish them.[45]

In an age when Western constituencies are bitterly divided by the demographics of education, religion, class, and urban versus rural populations, we need a confident pluralism more than ever before. We need a political framework that exhibits 'tolerance for dissent, a skepticism of government orthodoxy, and a willingness to endure strange and even offensive ways of life'.[46] We need to find a way to live with one another in spite of our differences and together strive to 'find and follow the way of peace, and discover how to build each other up'.[47] Victory in liberal democracy is not vanquishing our opponents, but winning their respect, living in peace with them, and affirming their right to their opinion. That means LGBTQ+ people have the right to be themselves, Muslims can be Muslims, and Christians can be Christians, Socialists can be Socialists, Greenies can be Greenies. We can disagree with what other people say, but only if we are willing to defend their right to be disagreeable. In the

---

43 Tim Wilson, 'Rediscovering Humility: freedom in a 21st century pluralist society', *Acton Lecture* 2, Centre for Independent Studies, 14 November 2016.

44 Alasdair MacIntyre, *After Virtue*, 2nd edn (Notre Dame, IN: University of Notre Dame Press, 1984), p. 253.

45 Galston, *Practice of Liberal Pluralism*, pp. 65–6.

46 Inazu, *Confident Pluralism*, p. 125.

47 Romans 14:19.

end, nobody has the right not to be offended, just as nobody has the right to silence criticism of their political perspective. What is more, 'If our culture cannot form people who speak with both conviction and empathy across deep differences,' claim John Inazu and Timothy Keller, 'then it becomes even more important for the church to use its theological and spiritual resources to produce such people.'[48]

Our age is one where there are post-liberal tendencies at all ends of the political spectrum. Some pundits and political powerbrokers believe that their opponents either should not be allowed to exist or should not be allowed to share their opinions. The dangers with post-liberal perspectives in the hands of governing authorities is that a government too insistent on promoting certain values can undermine liberty itself.[49] Good government arises from the cultivation of debate, not ritual denunciations or intimidation. Tolerance properly understood means 'the refusal to use coercive state power to impose one's views on others, and therefore a commitment to moral competition through recruitment and persuasion alone'.[50]

Liberal democracy allows diversity, which requires confidence in our institutions to manage differences within diversity in healthy ways. This includes, too, the tricky task of putting limits on the types of tolerable diversity (things such as female genital mutilation, polygamy or racial discrimination). In a politically pluralistic society, all people, irrespective of their convictions, are able to participate in our democratic system without fear of reprisal. The result is that you can have a situation, like that in the UK at the moment, where you have a Christian king, a Hindu prime minister, a Buddhist home secretary, a Muslim first minister of Scotland, and an atheist opposition leader. That type of pluralism creates peaceful participation in politics by people of all stripes. This pluralism is not the ultimate goal of Christian endeavours, but it is expedient for the promotion of the gospel and the practice of peace on earth.

---

48 John Inazu and Timothy Keller, 'Introduction', in *Uncommon Ground: Living faithfully in a world of differences* (Nashville, TN: Nelson, 2020), p. 16.

49 Stephen Macedo, *Diversity and Distrust: Civic education in a multicultural democracy* (Cambridge, MA: Harvard University Press, 2003), p. 146.

50 Galston, *Practice of Liberal Pluralism*, p. 4.

8

Conclusion

Lee C. Camp opened his book on Christianity and politics with a very provocative statement: 'The faith of the Christian is the last great hope of earth.'[1] That claim will raise the eyebrows of people who think that 'progress', economic growth, nuclear power, nuclear disarmament, population reduction, social justice, socialism, diplomacy, open borders, religious revival, religious decline or technology will be the saviour for humanity's problems. Yet we believe with prophetic fervour and patient endurance that God alone is the world's Redeemer and this redemption comes to us in Jesus and by renewal in the holy spirit. Such a view does not imply that we should abandon the world to other agencies, withdraw from worldly ventures, or even leave everything to God. No, such a view calls us to action because if there is to be a day when 'God may be all in all', then our energies are quickened, not stifled, so that the emerging task is to get busy in the business of the kingdom: 'always excelling in the work of the Lord, because you know that in the Lord your labour is not in vain.'[2] If our hope is in God and God's kingdom to be on earth as it is in heaven, then we are called to be disciples with a theo-political vision of the gospel, not advocates for a theocratic regime, nor withdrawn to the safety of our cloistered compound. The tension is that God's kingdom is for this world, but we do not build the kingdom ourselves; we only build for it. While our Christian labours remain in the domain of the 'not yet' of hopes for the fullness of the kingdom; we are neither passive nor paralysed in the interim. Instead, the imperatives of our kingdom-callings mean considering

---

1 Lee C. Camp, *Scandalous Witness: A little political manifesto for Christians* (Grand Rapids, MI: Eerdmans, 2020), p. 1.

2 1 Corinthians 15:28, 58.

how to bear Christ's name and to walk in his way amid the travail and tragedies of this age. A kingdom-perspective requires prophetic witness, priestly intercession and political discernment.

In this book, we have attempted to do a number of things related to the topics of political theology, public discipleship, Christian testimony in the face of tyranny, and debates over Church and State relationships.

First, we have recognised that the world we live in now is at a moment of social and economic turmoil, with new imperial powers rising and democratic nations tearing themselves apart. In such a combustible world, we need to think about political theology, both theory and practice, more acutely than since the Second World War. The urgency is not about the next election, the latest scandal or hot political issue; what is up for grabs is the place of Christians in the State and the type of state that Christians should support.

Second, we've observed that God's people have always had to deal with empires, from the many empires of the ancient Near East, to the empires of Greece and Rome, to Mongol and Muslim dominions. Jesus appeared in Galilee and Judaea when the Roman Empire seemed almost undefeatable. He was crucified, given a slave's death by an imperial governor. In the aftermath, his followers, those who later called themselves 'Christians', would be treated as either a rogue religious sect or else as enemies of the State by Roman authorities. But eventually, their witness would win Rome over, and Caesar himself would bow the knee to Jesus. At one level, this was a blessed relief; it meant the end of persecution, but it also led to the advent of Christendom, and a new and complex relationship between the Church and the State, complexities that have continuously evolved since the sixteenth century and that shape the socio-religious fabric of our current times.

Third, Christianity has always had a public witness, and our conception of the kingdom shapes how we relate to the political and social challenges of the day. Christianity revolutionised the Roman Empire, and transformed it from a hegemonic pagan power into a loose confederation of Christian realms in the West and in the East. While Christians had often been agents of resistance and revolution against empires, truth be told, at other times they were all too happy to act as chaplains of a christianised state. During the Middle Ages, the Church enjoyed the patronage and privileges that came from such an alliance between kings and bishops. It was precisely the close relationship between the Church and European powers, extending into religious wars and making Christians complicit with colonial violence, which might make us sceptical of mixing Christianity and politics. Be that as it may, to build for the kingdom means building something on earth that anticipates the new creation. Such witness and work does cross over into the political realm. Christian testimony must not shrink back from its theo-political implications, even if it must be vigilant not to be seduced by the temptations of proximity to political power.

Fourth, we laid out that governing authority is a God-given institution that, in part, carries forward the divine design for humans to be custodians of creation. Further, Jesus is both the conduit and model as to how divine authority flows into and transforms the human world. The problem is, unfortunately, that human authority is corrupted by the poisonous pursuit of power and contaminated by the human attachment to idols of every kind. A seduction that is enabled and was perhaps even started by dark and evil forces of the heavenly realm. The biblical story, climaxing in Jesus, is that God intends to put all the powers under Jesus, which means redeeming humans with divine love, healing creation through the spirit, and acknowledging Jesus as lord and judge over despots and demons alike. In the end, God's sovereignty, as well as human regency over nature, and even Israel's priestly vocation in the world – all of that is telescoped into Jesus. Accordingly, Jesus' followers, who will reign with him over the new creation, have the task now to prepare the world for the day when terror and tears are no more.

Fifth, we have argued too that the Church, meaning all practising Christians in reality, has a duty to bear public witness. Our job is not to build the kingdom on earth. Only God can do that. We have no misapprehensions about establishing a Christian utopia after one good revival or in the aftermath of a cathartic revolution. But we are to build *for* the kingdom, to prepare for it, to anticipate it, to turn our communities into signposts displaying it. That's why we are to pray that it will be on earth as it is heaven, to colonise earth with the life of heaven, to bear witness by declaring the gospel truth to all who listen, and speaking truth to political powers even when they refuse to listen. While Christians are called to public service, they are not called to wield absolute power. Christians must seek to serve, not dominate. That is because cross and kingdom go together. Christ is the ultimate power, yet he became a servant. He made the ultimate sacrifice; though he was in the form of God, he willingly died the death of a slave. Our lives, individually and corporately, should mirror sacrifice and service, as that is the best way to demonstrate what the kingdom of God will look like in all its fullness.

Sixth, we have explored how Christians should relate to governing authorities. We discovered in the New Testament that there is an oscillating perspective of submission to state authorities and at other times subversively resisting them. The same tension has carried over into church history all the way up to the present. The case was made that texts such as Romans 13:1–7 and 1 Peter 2:13–17 do not give carte blanche to government authorities. Disobedience to unjust government is possible since it is the institution of government, and not every individual governor, which deserves our obedience. Indeed, the Christian tradition is full of examples of civil disobedience, when a government orders people to do things against their religious convictions. Plus, Christians have often pondered what to do in the face of tyranny. How to pray, and whether to pursue courses of action to remove the tyrant even if it requires disobedience and civil war.

Seventh, there are many varieties of tyranny or unjust government that Christians may find the need to resist. The ones identified include totalitarian regimes, whether Fascist or Communist, Christian nationalism, and post-liberal civic totalism. Christian faith is an allegiance to King Jesus, and that allegiance often requires the Church to engage in active defiance of tyranny, cruelty, corruption and despotism.

Eighth, and finally, we have examined the very nature of state authority itself. We concluded that, while government is good, the authority of the state needs to be limited. No state apparatus should aspire to be all-powerful. In the quest for a good and just state, we have set forth the case for liberal democracy and an ethos of confident pluralism. We do not regard liberal democracy as uniquely Christian; neither is it perfect, infallible or beyond criticism. But liberal democracy and confident pluralism constitute a form of government and political philosophy that gives us the best opportunity to love God and to love our neighbour. It is a working arrangement to help us find unity even with our differences, to promote freedom and responsibility, and to pursue the things that make for peace and mutual encouragement. That way, everyone may sit under their own vine and fig tree, and no one shall make them afraid.[3]

---

3   Micah 4:4; Zechariah 3:10.

Index of Biblical References and Ancient Texts

OLD TESTAMENT

Genesis
1 *43, 48*
1:2 *47*
1:26–9 *84*
1:27 *156, 157, 167*
1:27–8 *43, 77*
1:28 *44*
2 *43, 48*
3 *45, 47*
3 – 11 *46, 57*
6:5–7 *46*
8 *48*
12 – 22 *48*
41:37–57 *98*

Exodus
9:16 *11*
19:6 *44, 99*
20:2 *11*
23:22 *44*

Leviticus
19:18 *159, 167*

Deuteronomy
1:13–15 *162*
28:58–68 *47*
32 *51*
32:16–17 *51*

Judges
17:6 *47, 161*

18:1 *47*
19:1 *47*
21:25 *47, 161*

1 Kings
1:39 *162*
21 *xi*

2 Kings
22:14–20 *98*

1 Samuel
4:1–22 *70*
8:4–18 *47*
13:14 *47*

2 Samuel
2:4 *162*
7 *48*
7:12–16 *47*

Psalms
2 *48*
2:1 *15*
2:1–11 *11*
2:2 *131*
2:9 *49*
8 *43, 84, 98*
8:1 *44*
8:4 *44*
8:5–6 *44*
8:6 *84, 85*
8:9 *44*
9 *103*

9:5 *103*
9:7–8 *103*
22:28 *5*
31 *89*
37:11 *66*
72 *48, 64, 73*
72:4 *49*
72:19 *49*
82:8 *7*
110:5–6 *49*
132 *48*
137:3–4 *12*

Proverbs
8:15 *152*
8:15–16 *110*
21:1 *152*

Isaiah
9:2–7 *50*
10 *43*
11:1–10 *49, 50, 62*
11:9 *62*
11:10 *21, 61*
14 *51*
14:3–21 *15*
14:12–23 *51*
40 – 45 *59*
42:1–9 *50*
45:1 *131*
45:1–2 *14*
45:1–13 *130*
45:12–13 *14*
49:1–13 *50*

50:4–9 *50*
52 *12*
52 – 53 *80*
52:1–10 *13*
52:7 *14*
52:13 – 53:12 *50*
53 *14*
59: 7 *xi*
61:1–11 *50*
63:1–6 *50*

Jeremiah
4:23 *47*
9 *11*
29:7 *98*

Daniel
2 *98*
2:21 *5, 152*
2:44–7 *16*
3:17–18 *113*
4 *98*
5 *98*
5:1–31 *16*
7 *51*
7:1–8 *14*
7:1–28 *51*
7:8 *15, 49*
7:13–14 *15*
7:25 *49*
7:27 *49*

Hosea
8:4 *115*

179

Micah
4:4 *38, 178*

Habakkuk
1:2 *12*
2:3–4 *12*
3:18 *12*

Zechariah
3:10 *38, 178*

APOCRYPHA
1 Maccabees
  2:68 *113*
2 Maccabees 9:12
  15
Sirach 10.4 *110*

NEW TESTAMENT

Matthew
2:1–10 *140*
4:15 *128*
4:17–19 *81*
4:23 *82*
5:5 *66*
5:38–9 *117*
5:43 *159*
5:43–8 *160*
6:10 *9*
10:16 *90*
10:32–3 *108*
11:5 *19*
12:28 *19, 82*
12:32 *71*
13:33 *91*
19:19 *159*
22:39 *159*
20:16 *127*
20:28 *80*
26:53 *136*
27:36–7 *81*
28:18 *73, 97*

Mark
1:15 *19*
2:1–12 *82*
8:38 *108*
9:1 *19*
10:42 *91*
10:45 *80*
10:46–7 *82*
14:53–65 *82*

Luke
1:52–3 *126*
4:18 *149*
7:1–10 *105*
7:11–17 *82*
7:22–3 *19*
10:25–37 *160*
11:20 *19*
12:8–9 *108*
23 *106*

John
1:1–3 *45*
1:14 *45*
3:16 *157*
6:15 *136*
8:32 *149*
12 *57*
12:23 *54*
12:27 *54*
12:31–2 *42, 54*
13 *54*
13:2 *54*
13:30 *54*
14:30 *54*
16:2 *71*
16:8–11 *63*
16:33 *42, 54*
17:14–16 *97*
18:3 *54*
18:36 *35, 71*
19 *54*
19:5 *44*

19:10–11 *110*
19:11 *42*
20 – 21 *55*

Acts of the Apostles
2:22–36 *82*
2:44–5 *125*
2:47 *106*
3:1–10 *82*
3:12–26 *82*
3:13 *106*
4:1–21 *82*
4:8–12 *82*
4:19 *74*
4:25–6 *15*
4:27 *106*
4:32 *125*
5:29 *75, 101, 106*
5:37 *18*
8:12 *82*
9:32–5 *82*
9:36–43 *82*
10:21–7 *105*
10:34–46 *82*
10:36 *106*
12:1–2 *107*
13:4–13 *106*
13:28 *106*
17:6 *27*
17:7 *101, 106, 140*
17:26 *29, 156*
18:12–16 *106*
19:30–1 *105*
24:26 *106*
25:11–12 *105*
26:26–9 *63*

Romans
1:3–5 *62*
5:17 *44*
5:18–19 *19*
8 *51*

8:18–30 *62*
8:29 *19*
8:38–9 *51*
12:17 *117*
13 *100, 167*
13:1–3 *108*
13:1–5 *98, 109, 120*
13:1–7 *20, 105, 115, 152, 153, 177*
13:9–10 *159*
14 *61*
14:19 *172*
15 *68*
15:7–13 *62*
15:8 *19*
15:12 *21*
15:13 *62*

1 Corinthians
6:2–3 *63*
7:4 *29*
15:3 *19*
15:20 *19*
15:24 *19*
15:24–8 *85*
15:27–8 *84*
15:28 *9, 77, 174*
15:58 *85, 174*

2 Corinthians
3:17 *149*
5:5 *19*
8:13–14 *125*

Galatians
3:27–9 *67*
3:28 *28*
4:26 *61*
5:1 *149*
5:6 *7*
5:14 *159*

Index of Biblical References and Ancient Texts

Ephesians
1:10 57, 69, 85
1:13 19
1:21 51
2:11–22 57, 69
3:10 68

Philippians
2:10–11 100
3:20–1 98

Colossians
1 50, 55
1:12–17 40
1:15–16 56, 59
1:17–18a 56
1:18 19
1:18b–20 56, 59
1:19 45
2 57
2:9 45
2:13–15 59
2:14–15 57
3 67
3:10–11 67
3:12–17 68
4:11 9

1 Thessalonians
4:3–6 29

1 Timothy
1:10 29
2:2 7

2 Timothy
2:1 84, 98
2:12 77
6:12–13 108

Philemon
16 29

Hebrews
2:5–9 84
2:7–9 85
2:8 98

James
2:8 159

1 Peter
2:9 99
2:13–17 105, 109, 152, 153, 177

Revelation
1:6 44, 99
2:10 7
5 59
5:10 44, 84, 99
7 68
7:9–12 59
11:15 16, 41, 98
11:18 15
13 107
20 107
20:6 44
21:1 77
22:5 84

CHRISTIAN LITERATURE

Apostolic Fathers
1 Clement 60.4 – 61.3 7

Epistle to Diognetus
5.2 77
5.4 77
6.1 78

Martyrdom of Polycarp
9.3 108

10.2 108

Polycarp,
   Epistle to the Philippians
12.3 7

Athenagoras
Plea for the Christians
37 7

Augustine
City of God
19.17 78
19.19 77
19.20 78

Chrysostom, John
Homilies on 2 Corinthians
16 95

Homilies on 2 Thessalonians
4 95

Homilies on Romans
24 112

Eusebius
Church History
3.19–20 35

Oration in the Praise of Constantine
16.4 95

Gregory of Nyssa
Homilies on Ecclesiastes
4 125

Justin
First Apology
11 35
12 106

Origen
Against Celsus
3.44 26
3.5–10 22
8.2 21
8.73 7, 106

Tertullian
Apology
4 114
30.4 7
30–4 106
31.2 7

GRECO-ROMAN SOURCES

Horace
Satires
1.2.116–19 29

Inscriptions
Sylloge Inscriptionum Graecarum
814.30–1 20

Josephus
Jewish Antiquities
17.271–2 18
17.285–91 19
17.286–98 18

Index of Biblical References and Ancient Texts

18.23–5 *18*
20.200 *107*

Jewish War
2.55–6 *18*
2.66–79 *18*
2.68–71 *19*
2.118 *18*
2.140 *110*
2.433 *18*

Suetonius
Vespasian
4.4 *20*

Tacitus
Agricola
30 *17*

Histories
5.13 *20*

MEDIEVAL SOURCES

Isidore of Seville
Sentences
3.51 *133*

John of Salisbury
Policraticus
4.1 *114*
8.18–20 *114*

John Wycliffe
Civil Lordship 115

Thomas Aquinas
Commentary on the Sentences
44.2.2 *115*

On Kingship
1.6 *115*

REFORMED THEOLOGY

Calvin, John
Institutes
4.20.2 *133*
4.20.8 *159*
4.20.9 *152*
4.20.10 *161*
4.20.11 *152*
4.20.29 *113*
4.20.31 *113*
4.20.32 *111*

Lectures on Daniel
6.22 *111*

Turretin, Francis
Institutes of Elenctic Theology
3.316–36 *133*

Westminster Confession of Faith
23.3 *133*

CATHOLIC ENCYCLICALS

Centesimus Annus 117, 127

Evangelium Vitae 161

Index of Names

Ahdar, Rex 137
Alexander, Laura E. 146

Bacelli, Bruno 159
Bacote, Vincent 91, 150
Bailey, David C. 116
Barnes, Timothy D. 95
Ben Sirach 110
Berlinerblau, Jacques 91
Biggar, Nigel 32
Bird, Michael F. 8, 19, 22, 43, 91, 109, 136, 171
Blair, Tony 74, 76, 131
Bockmuehl, Klaus 142
Bonhoeffer, Dietrich 119, 128
Bowens, Lisa M. 30
Brennan, Jason 117
Bretherton, Luke 30, 91, 137, 160, 167, 168
Brooks, David 138
Bush, George H. 136

Calvin, John 111, 113, 114
Câmara, Hélder Pessoa 126
Cameron, David 75, 76
Camp, Lee C. 112, 174
Campbell, Alastair 74
Chadwick, Owen 94
Chan, Simon 128
Charles III, King 40, 72, 130
Chatraw, Joshua D. 91
Chenoweth, Erica 117
Chesterton, G. K. 143
Chiang Kai-Shek 103, 104
Churchill, Winston 103

Cole, Jonathan 166, 168
Constantine, Emperor 130
Cross, F. L. 95

Dalrymple, William 32, 166
Davison Hunter, James 93
De Gaulle, Charles 103
Delmas, Candice 118
Dewey, John 139
Dickson, John 31
Doyle, Andrew 142
Drant, Will 23
Dwight, John Sullivan 39
Dyson, R. W. 133

Edwards, Jonathan 33
Eliot, T. S. 167
Elizabeth II, Queen 130
Elkins, Caroline 121
Ellul, Jacques 5, 123, 128, 163
Embery, Paul 138

Falwell, Jerry 136
Fantin, Joseph D. 20
Fowden, Elizabeth Key 31
Fox, Jonathan 141
Frazer, Gregg L. 116
Fukuyama, Francis 3, 4, 5

Galston, Wiliam A. 139, 160, 172, 173
Gitari, David 21
Gibbon, Edward 28
Goodwin, Matthew 138
Gottwald, Klement 163
Grudem, Wayne 163

Index of Names

Grundmann, Walter 127, 128

Habermas, Jurgen 141
Halík, Tomáš 118, 124
Hall, S. G. 125
Hamid, Shadi 167
Harris, John W. 30
Hart, David Bentley 159, 163
Hass, Peter J. 124
Hauerwas, Stanley 5, 33, 34
Heise, Matthew 128
Hengel, Martin 21, 112
Hitler, Adolf 70, 120, 124, 163
Holland, Tom 27, 28, 103, 126, 143, 144
Hooker, Richard 106
Horrell, David G. 110
Horsley, R. H. 2

Inazu, John D. 171, 172, 173

Jensen, Peter 153
John Chrysostom 112
John Paul II, Pope 145
Johnson, Ben 38
Justin Martyr 105

Kalantzis, George 121
Käsemann, Ernst 149
Keck, Leander E. 109
Keesmaat, S. 68
Kelaidis, K. 70, 136
Keller, Timothy 173
King, Martin Luther 92, 96, 99, 131, 133
Kinzig, Wolfram 107
Kirill, Patriarch 136
Kisis, Konstantin 34
Kwarteng, Kwasi 32
Kwok Pui-Lan 10, 147, 148, 169
Kyounghan, Bae 104

Lee, Gregory W. 121

Leigh, Ian 137
Leithart, Peter 34, 140
Leopold, King 124
Lenski, Noel 31
Lévy, Bernard-Henri 140, 142
Liebeschuetz, J. H. W. G. 95
Livingstone, E. A. 95
Lloyd-Jones, Martyn 12
Locke, John 133, 134, 142
Lockwood O'Donovan, Joan 94, 114, 115, 130, 133, 158,163

McAnnally-Linz, Ryan 115
Macedo, Stephen 139, 140, 141, 173
MacIntyre, Alasdair 172
Mao Zedong 124
Mason, Rowena 75
Middleton, J. R. 46
Milbank, John 130
Milton, John 115
Mitter, Rana 103
More, Hannah 30
Motyl, Alexander J. 32
Mounk, Yascha 138

Nation, Hannah 129
Niebuhr, Reinhold 97, 162
Niemoller, Martin 128
Nongbri, B. 70

O'Donovan, Oliver 31, 76, 94, 114, 115, 130, 131, 133, 143, 158, 163
Orwell, George 126

Paine, Thomas 142
Perrin, Nicholas 8
Pierce, Joseph 120
Pinker, Steven 28
Prior, Karen Swallow 91
Putin, Vladimir 4, 70, 136

Ramsey, Michael 93, 94
Rawls, John 118, 119

Index of Names

Romero, Oscar 128
Rutherford, Samuel 115

Sattler, Michael 107
Saunders, Benjamin 119
Schiess, Kaitlyn 120
Schreiner, Thomas R. 110
Siedentop, Larry 158
Simpson, James 158
Shelley, Percy Bysshe 16
Skillen, James W. 77
Smith, James K. A. 31, 92, 94, 143, 144, 146, 158
Smith, Steven D. 141
Snyder, Timothy 124, 129, 169
Solzhenitsyn, Aleksandr 127
Song, C. S. 128
Stalin, Josef 124
Stark, R. 64
Stephen, Maria J. 117
Steward, Gary L. 116
Stout, Jeffrey 92, 137
Sunak, Rishi 40

Taleb, Nassim Nicholas 26, 27
Taylor, Charles 127
Temple, William 97
Thomas Aquinas 115, 133
Tolkien, J. R. R. 159
Treat, Jeremy R. 79

Truman, Harry S. 103
Trump, Donald 130
Tseng, J. D. 129
Turner, Gerald 118

Vallier, Kevin 134
VanDrunen, David 119
Verhofstadt, Guy 37

Walsh, B. 68
Wang Yi 129
West, Cornel 168
Whitfield, George 33
Wilberforce, William 92, 99
Williams, Olivia R. 120
Williams, Travis B. 110
Willimon, William H 5, 33
Wilson, Tim 172
Wink, W. 51
Witte, John 158
Wojtyla, Karol 116
Wolterstorff, Nicholas 108, 111, 114, 135, 153, 156
Woodberry, Robert D. 158
Wright, N T 5, 7, 8, 14, 19, 21, 22, 23, 36, 45, 52, 55, 56, 58, 59, 61, 62, 70, 71, 78, 79, 81, 104, 109, 145,
Wycliffe, John 115

Yong, Amos 92